FROM AN ANTIQUE LAND

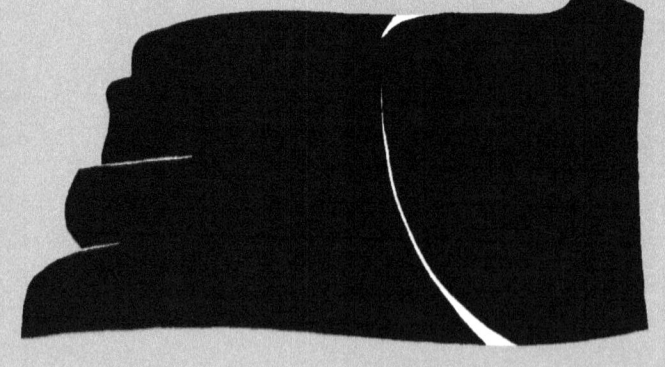

FROM AN ANTIQUE LAND

Fred Martin

Green Gates Press

Second Edition

Drawn by Fred Martin
with technical assistance
by Benjamin Cavalcanti

Green Gates Press
#116, 4096 Piedmont Avenue
Oakland, CA 94611, USA

ISBN 978-0-578-01199-8

For The Reader

Note:

The content of this book derives from a series of experiments with altered states of consciousness which I undertook under the guidance of the Monroe Institude of Applied Sciences during 1977 and 1978. By the use of a special audio beat, a frequency following response around seven cycles per second was spread and synchronized over wide areas of my brain. Post-hypnotic techniques were used so that this state could be achieved later at will. Using the special state of consciousness called Focus 10, which arises parallel to the physiological condition stimulated by the audio beat, I received preliminary training in most of the fundamental parapsychological phenomena, including clairvoyance, telepathy, psychic healing, and developing the awareness of what in other similar disciplines is called perception and strengthening of the etheric body.

From the base of Focus 10, which is primarily a parapsychological approach to physical reality, I was introduced to a second state of altered consciousness called Focus 12. This state provided a way for the expansion of my consciousness, first into out of body travel in the physical world, and second for perception/experience on the "non-physical planes of being." These latter perceptions and experiences were my primary goal in undertaking the Monroe Training, and they form the chief body of material in this book.

Focus 12 can be expanded in turn to what the Monroe Institute refers to as Focus 15, a state of consciousness where time does not exist and where, perhaps, the direct perception takes place of what in this book I have called "God."

Someone asked me once when I read him a part of the manuscript, if I believed all that is in it. I could only reply, "It happened."

These are leaves from a great and un-
known tree. They fall sometimes singly in
the silence of long afternoons, sometimes
in torrents with the winds of evening,
sunset, dawn. They are fragments from
another land.

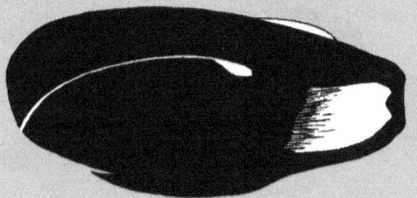

I met a traveler from an antique land who said...

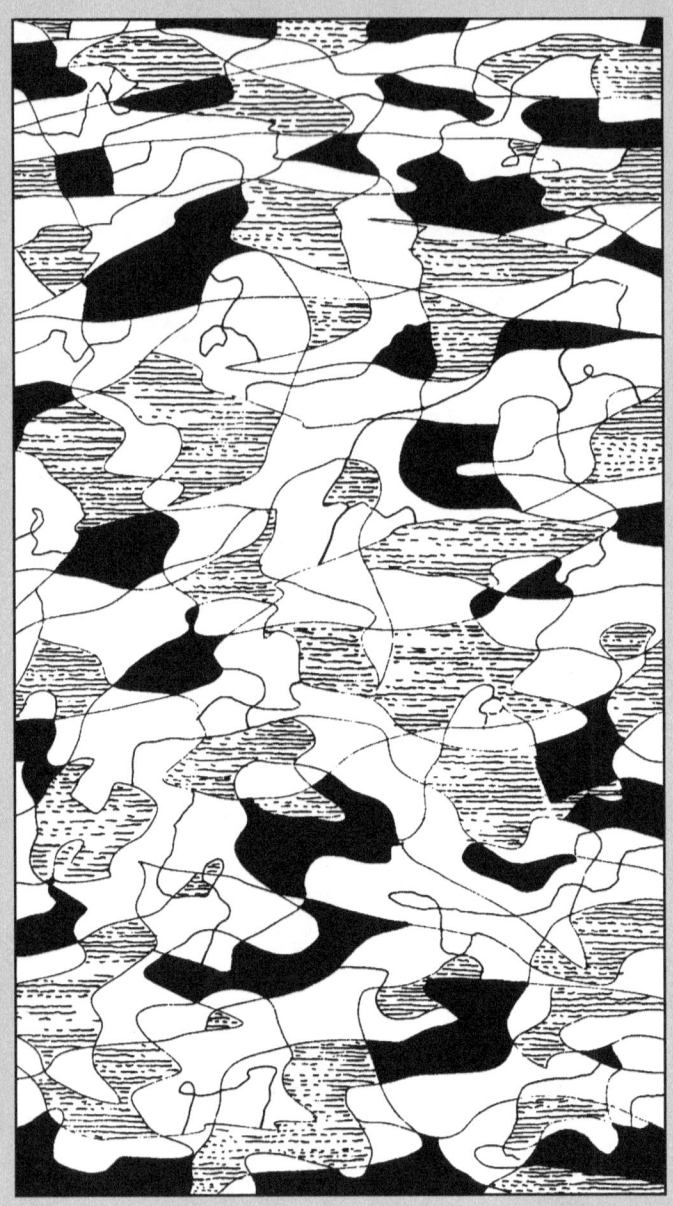

IT IS ALL ONE TISSUE and we are nodes in it, tiny knots in a white and seething skein of energy.

In the infinite tissue of mind which is God, points occur which move matter into the pattern of the sperm cell and the ovum, which move sperm and ovum to find each other and the body to be born, which move the long gathering of matter around the body through every phase from birth until death, and which move all the material world that is clustered around the body in the infinite tissue of the mind of God.

Hence we are mortal because the matter which we are will disperse when the point of mind no longer shapes it; hence we are immortal because the points of mind which we are, are one with the infinite tissue of the whole of which we are so small a part. Hence the reality of the soul of each of us. Hence our sense of the oneness of the world in energy, and of the world's multitudinous dispersal in matter. Hence our ability to communicate with one another by sensory means as our minds shape the matter to be read that was shaped by other minds, and our ability to communicate extrasensorily, by the shared vibrations of the infinite tissue of mind. Hence clairvoyance, as we shift from place to place along the endless fibers of that tissue. And hence our changeful dreams, as we perceive upon the planes of different rates of vibration in the one, infinitely vibrating tissue of mind.

2. **T**HE OLD TEXT SAID, "The physical body for a journey in the physical world, the soul for a journey in the world of spirit."

*

I lay beside a mountain lake. As I looked along my body, I could see the peaks beyond the lake touched with red pink light, and I sensed the dawn sun rising in clear yellow behind my head.

I became a large, egg shaped pearl of autumnal light floating in the gate of a castle of cloud, and then I was above the clouds, looking at the evening sun bright and clear on the horizon, seeing its rays turning, pulsing, swelling. And then it pulsed so greatly that the disc of the sun itself burst upon my forehead, its rays spreading all out and down the surface of my body; and it pulsed and pulsed there on the upper center of my forehead and it was the Lord and his rays poured down me like electric fire. And then I ate the pearl of autumn light that I had been and my body was filled with the Lord-light of the sun; the pearl and the sun were one in me.

I was at the height, facing up into the star world. The sun was setting very far back and to the right below. The star world reached out over me and flashes streamed down from its crown to the cardinal points.

*

And then the old text said, "Now your soul is free to take its far journey as you may desire."

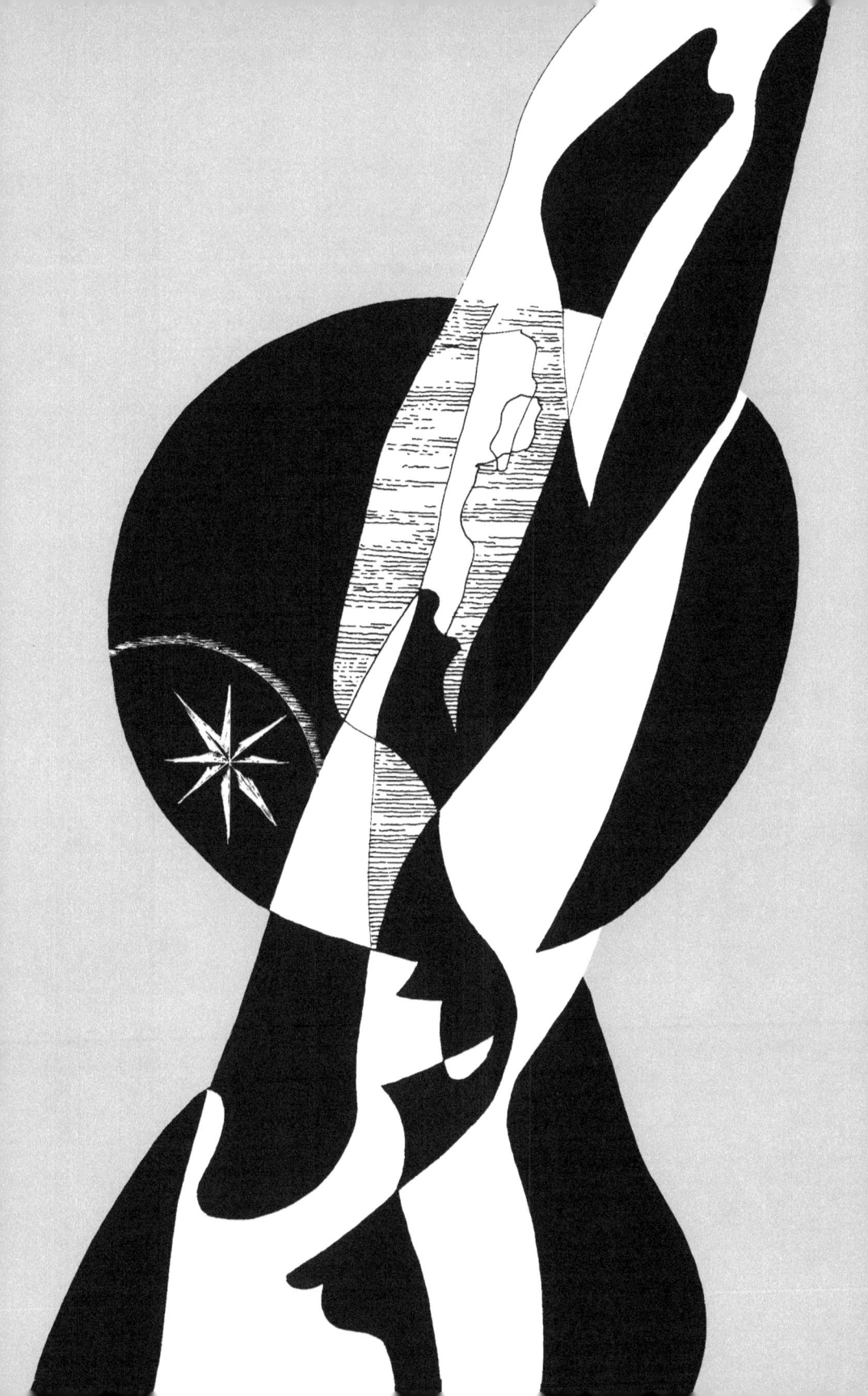

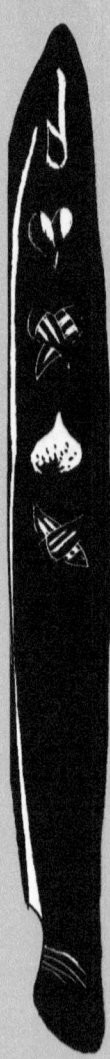

3. THEY TOOK A STREAM OF WHITE light and sent it looping throughout my body, concentrating it after a while on my genitals until my genitals became shining gold and white wings leapt out from the head of my phallus. Then my phallus grew up my body and curved over my shoulder and down my back and then up again between my legs until the white wings of it held my heart like open hands might hold an egg. They concentrated the light on my heart until it was red and shaped like my testicles; my heart bled a bit until white wings shot up from it also. They said I must join my genitals with my heart, and set me to sewing and lacing the two together with great looping threads of light. I put the genitals in back and the heart in front. The phallus curved down forward across the top of the heart; the heart's wings folded up and around the phallus.

The image was engraved on topaz. They touched it to my forehead, mounted it on a ring, and gave it to me as passport in their realm.

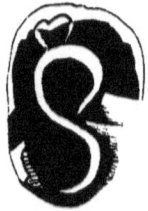

Through all my travels in the antique land, they guided me and spoke to me. They told me what actions I must take and took for me those actions of which I was not capable.

Once, they took my spine from my body and plunged the end of it into the sun, and then they

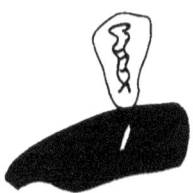

applied that white hot end to my body, as the lower half of my body plunged into the sun and my whole body floated upright, half white gold from being dipped in the sun. Waves of light flowed from both ends of in my spine like waves of energy; the waves crested at the center and my whole body was a tube with waves of light pouring from top and bottom toward the center, standing and peaking at the center. Then they whipped my whole body around and around in a spinning, coiling snake of light, finally pulling all light from me and driving it as a great snake in through my mouth, down my throat and into my gullet, my entrails, my groin. They rolled and double-coiled the snake of light there in the cup of my pelvis and then they lifted it back up the center of my body to sprout folded wings that were black with feathers tipped with white at the wing tips inside of my shoulders.

They looked at what they had done and said it was right.

*T*HEY SAID, "You have two brothers. We want you to meet them." They told 4. me the first was named Nurse Billy for the goat he is, and that he is also called Black Redmon for his hair and armor and blood. They said the second brother is named Ikarion for that young man who flew to the sun and who, contrary to legend, did not fall but lives there yet burning and shining and spinning through the sky.

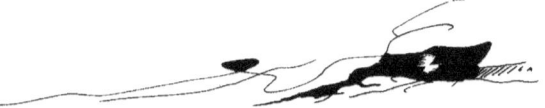

They put me in a weatherworn old shack by the sea. It was late afternoon, and the western sun reached through spray-dim windows to touch two caskets. The lid of one casket was marked with a red smear, the other was lidless and held only a few bits of turquoise and scraps of feathers. I lay on a cot in the shack and listened to the long pounding of the surf below. I watched the sun's slow warming of the wooden caskets and knew I was Black Redmon, I lay on the sand and a white man lay beside me. We licked each other and he was my beloved's vagina from which I drank and drank. With every breath I took I became Black Redmon; and as the strange light of that place began to fill my belly and limbs, it filled his.

I was a mummy case smeared with red and filled with light, and then I was a sizzling sphere, an egg of very bright silver spinning very rapidly indeed. Then

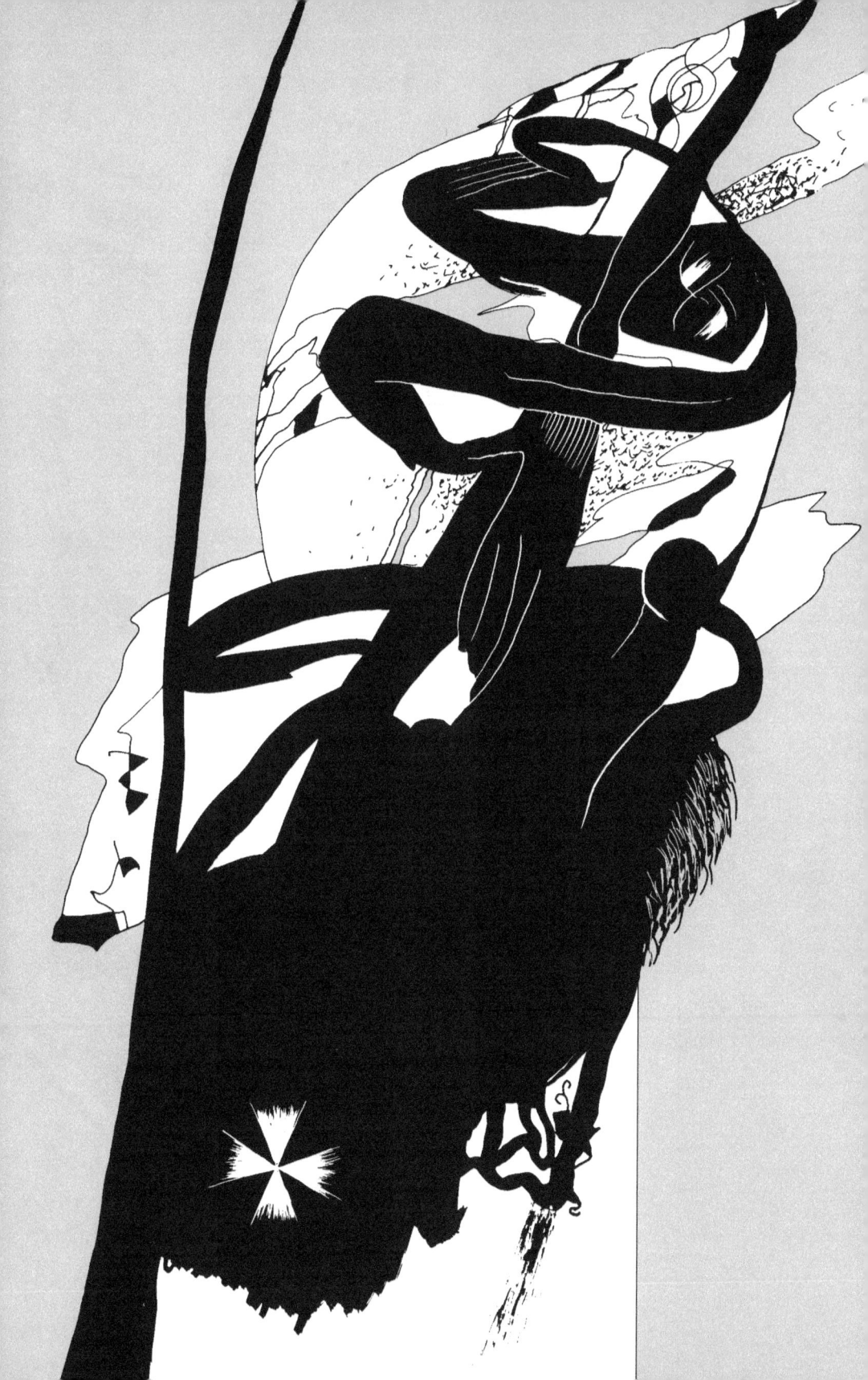

Ikarion leapt up hatched from the spinning egg in a winging frenzy of gold and turquoise fluttering every way. He was attached to the egg by strands of light, and he was high, high in the air and I saw him and was him.

He knelt and looked down to where he had come from while I calmed and stilled him so I could see how many wings he had; and then he stood at the same time and in the same place and opened his arms and wings and stretched them wide. And I looked at that opening and stretching several times, looked long and sweet.

And then Ikarion descended back into the seething silver egg that I had been and the egg descended into Black Redmon, and then I and my brothers were given for promise a vision of my beloved's vagina as a pine tree wound with white ribbons.

Later I learned that my brother Redmon is Pan, a satyr, a hunter, a warrior, an executioner and devil. I learned that he lives in the genitals and they are his sign. And I learned how to roll up to Ikarion in the sky, to be embraced in his wings of blue and gold, to eat into him, to crawl into his helmet, to enter in and to be with him.

5. I WAS WALKING among the hills on a late afternoon in early summer. I saw the turn of a fence ahead around the left

side of a hill above me; I saw the grass blowing in the afternoon sun, and in the sky I saw Ikarion's brothers marching in columns sweeping from horizon to zenith. I saw Ikarion's palace too, far out over the sea beyond the land.

I went near the zenith to meet his brothers who are also mine; I went to enter his palace by its distant gates to speak with him if I could. I lay on the steps of his great house until the winds took me to the top where the brothers were in the sky beyond. Their great white stallions marched and the winds carried me in that cavalcade up to the very eye of Ikarion himself, the sun gleaming among puddled clouds. I was pressed in and was flooded with Ikarion's eye and mind. His brain is a clotted skein of sperm and azure; it blazed and I ate it.

But Ikarion is only a sublunary god; and so at last I was swept up beyond him to where the sky is always night and clouds and stars stream like wings on each side of the moon.

Later, I went down to feed again from the light dimming now in Ikarion's eye, and to watch night fall everywhere among the sky's far, cloudy palaces.

*

Black Redmon and Ikarion were both gods in the beginning. Black Redmon was earth, night, Pan, male, animal and very serene and strong; Ikarion was sky, day, Mercury, male/female, fluttering, swooping, flashing. They are my brothers and God is above us, He upon whom I feed when I am Redmon and Ikarion.

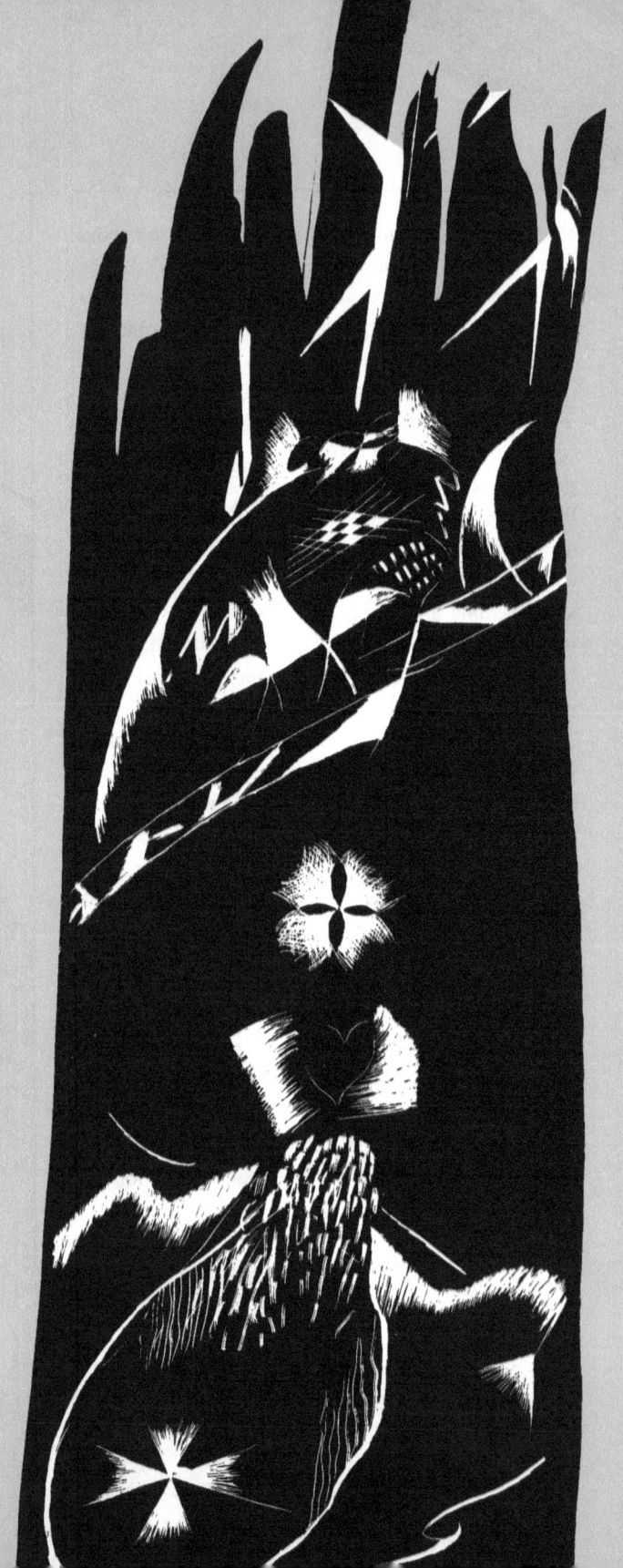

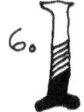**6.** FOUND A CORE OF LIGHT which was a cross at the base of my belly, and veils of light were drifting up from it throughout my body. With every inhalation the energy flowed through my body to that core and was caught. As I held my breath the cross spun and energy ran up the axis to my heart where it spun again as a blaze of blue light; then it ran up inside my skull where it stayed and swelled like electric fire. With every exhalation the energy poured down from the top of my head as a spherical shower of light around me.

There was a battle in a castle. I saw the flags, the gate, the men and weapons. I took out from my body that spinning axis of power. It was a fire stick made of iron and silver of Celtic and Medieval and Scythian work. It was cruel and sharp, and I spun and spun it between my hands, looking carefully at the center knob and the fiercely horned animal at the top with a crystal globe in its jaws. I used the stick as a sword, a battle axe, a mace, and began to carve my body with the lines of its force. My foot had four claws and I had but one leg to stand upon because the other was wrapped around it. My abdomen was a grid of diagonal slices, my chest was a double spiral, my arms were partially wings and my head was a silver globe set on my shoulders. I looked around at the castle and the battle and the snowy mountains far beyond and I knew all this was me and took it into my body for "This thou art."

I HELD A WHITE SWORD FOUNTAIN upright and light ran down over my hand. I was a faun, I was Pan. And I was Black Redmon, the hunter warrior in the armor of steel and fur and horns, holding a broadsword of bright crystal. It was engraved but the glare of light from it blinded me to the markings. I laid the crystal sword in a wooden coffin carved from a single log. Then I was the log, and the stream of light from the sword rose through me to flow down around me like a shining sphere.

7.

I saw the light rise from the sphere like a ladder or a road or a vine to heaven, and I saw the steps of my way as nodes or buds or translucent spheres in the stream of rising light. I looked around and saw everywhere a gently swaying pale blue tissue with the nodes of all the souls in it. I remembered the souls of the dead and knew that these were they, and I knew, since mine was there too and I'm alive now, that when I'm dead it will still be there and so what will be the difference?

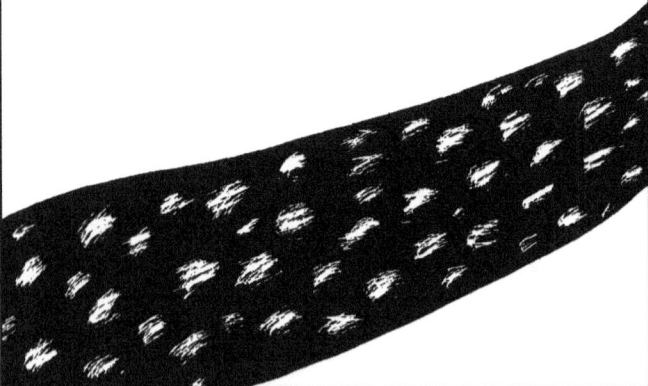

8. **I** FOUND FOUR SILVER BALLS in my pelvis; one at the front, the others at the back and the sides. There were silver fibers braiding from them up my spine and around my heart, around and down my shoulders like the veins of hooded wings, and on up into my head where they sprayed out inside the base of my skull. With every inhalation, energy came into the system; each time I held my breath it pulsed throughout the system to enlarge the wings and give life to the heart; and with every exhalation it sprayed blue light into my skull.

I saw a meadow high on the flank of Tamalpais in the early morning as the sun was breaking through the fog, and I saw an old, wooden watertank there and the light gleaming in the dripping overflow. I drank the bright drops one by one as pearls of light, and I drank the mist swirling brightly at the top of the fog fading before the sun.

The white light of the dawning sun crackled along the curve of the far horizon and crackled also across the underside of the top of my skull; it poured down the center of my brain like a crystallizing liquid, like a bright yellow morning sun gleaming among branches of distant trees; and it poured down into my shoulders/ wings and heart as the gold of cirrus in afternoon and the blue-red of horizons far across an ocean at twilight; and it poured down into my genitals and filled my erect phallus with the star-struck radiance of night.

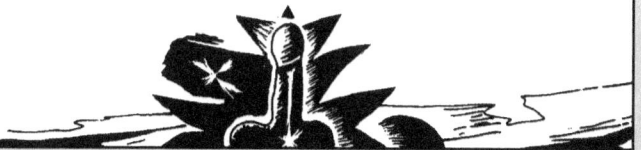

I found the ball again at the center of my pelvis, and I began to breathe the energy in through my legs and up in to the ball. Then I let the energy lift through my heart to the base of my skull where it expanded as clear, cerulean space in my head. The ball began to spin around the base of my spine as I lifted the energy again and again through the ever more towering core within me. The current flowed around and through my heart in white flames; it flowed upward into my head as electric fire.

I wished for this evening's sunset on Tamalpais, and I went there to perch on high rocks overhanging the sea and the sky. The late, orange sun flooded my head and it became my upper skull; it ran down my feathered face and hooked, sharp beak, it ran down my neck ... I was blue and amber with the red of sunset running down over me. The sun and air poured down my body and I saw my phallus, large and black. Thinking, suddenly, "I never know what to do with this," I knew I was a falcon, a bird of prey floating above the fog in an azure sky, between the mountain and the sea.

*

I was high in the dome of the sky where all the threads of the world are brought and their loose ends braided into the chain that leads to the great round window, the white circle of God. I climbed the rope and clambered in the window as God's white radiance poured on me. But I could not stay, and the window became an oval, failing like a tear-drop on a chain, like a drop of ivory-pearl down on me.

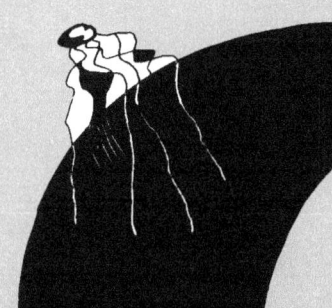

30. I WAS WALKING on the mountain in the autumn landscape. My blood tingled with tiny bubbles of clear blue and pale autumnal rose. I stood on a path by a rotting stump and saw ahead of me the old wooden water tank, dripping eternally in the meadow. My body became flooded with the sexual urge of golden-winged Ikari-on, his feathers covered me everywhere. He is Ikari-on-Captain, he is my phallus and I am he.

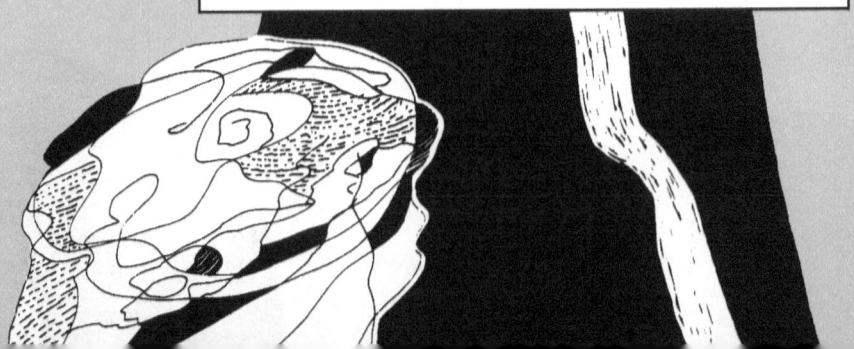

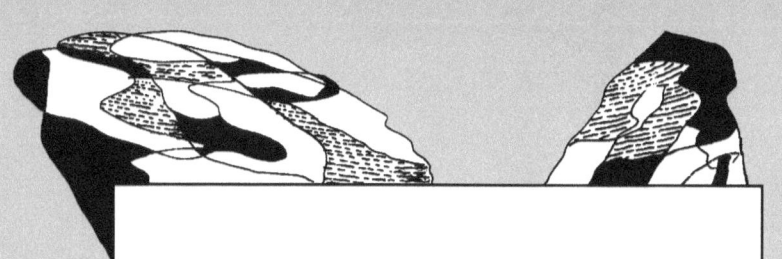

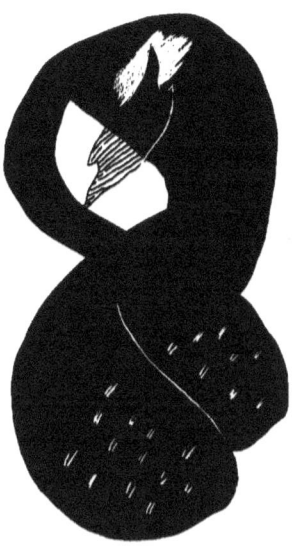

10. THE LIGHT SPUN DOWN through my body from head to foot, slowly replacing my physical body with another one that was lighter and filled with light.

I became lighter and lighter and went with the clouds ever higher into the sun, into the eye of the sun. The clouds were Ikarion's wild brothers on their stallions, and they were towers lifted very high into the great bowl of the sky. The sun glinted from the furthest horizon far down in a crack between the clouds, and I rode in a tower of cloud and saw the sun far away below.

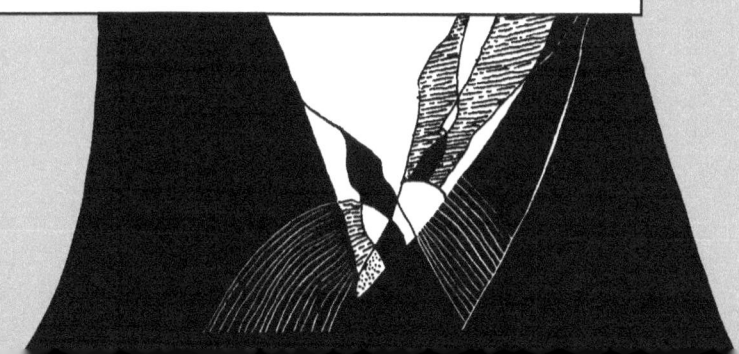

THE GATHERING PLACE was on the mountain far on the horizon, and I was 11. so high that I could see the world curve away and away and the sun very far down beyond, a tiny red ball in a pale ochre sky. The peaks of the mountain were old men sitting around a circle that was a lens or a tube sunk into the center at the top of the mountain.

I was given an instrument of brass and forced me to look up beyond the peaks to the place where there is no time, no time at all, where the moon and sun were in their conjunction, the curve of the sun just shining like a white crescent beyond the upper edge of the moon. I was told the instrument of brass was made for seeing this and is marked with a horizontal division to separate the above and below of the conjunction. I saw a tiny dot of darkness high on the crescent of the sun, and I was sent to see it close up and look higher and higher. And then the crescent of white sunlight at the top of the dark disc of the moon was driven down through all the length of my body, and then it was driven again down all through me.

Later, below, I sat with the old men that were the peaks of the mountain and we watched the sun going down. Even later, down in the valley in the twilight, I looked up at the last light among the crags.

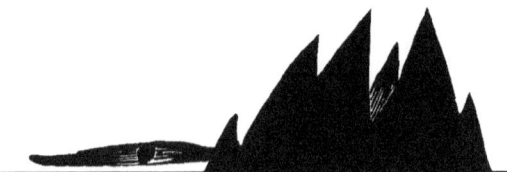

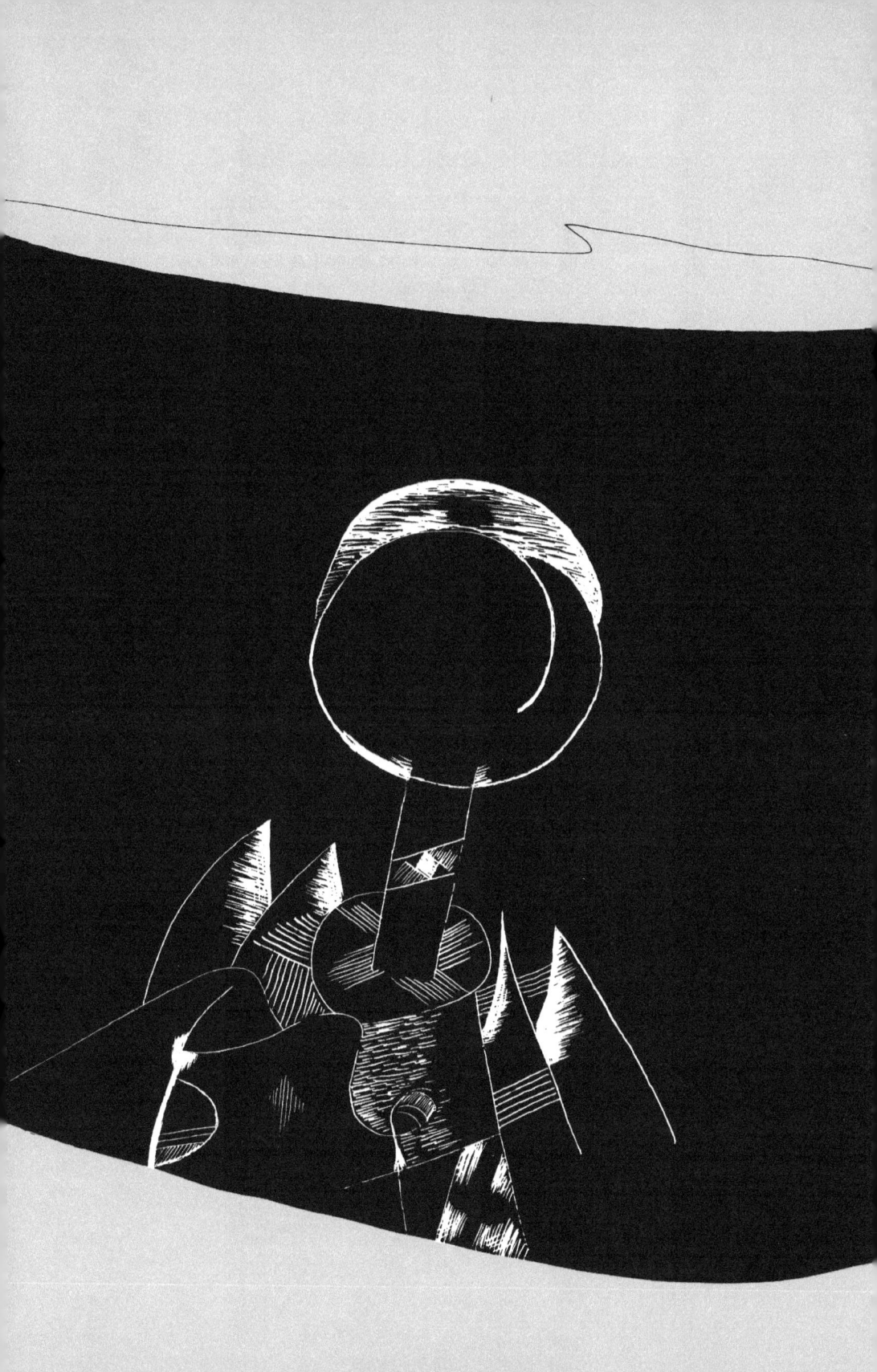

ASKED TO SEE the lens that reveals the highest, farthest and most real because I 12. wanted to know the deepest, nearest and most true. I found the lens at last when I looked out through the back of my head and saw there the fruits of the Tree of Life. Then I knew that the experience of life is the lens that reveals God.

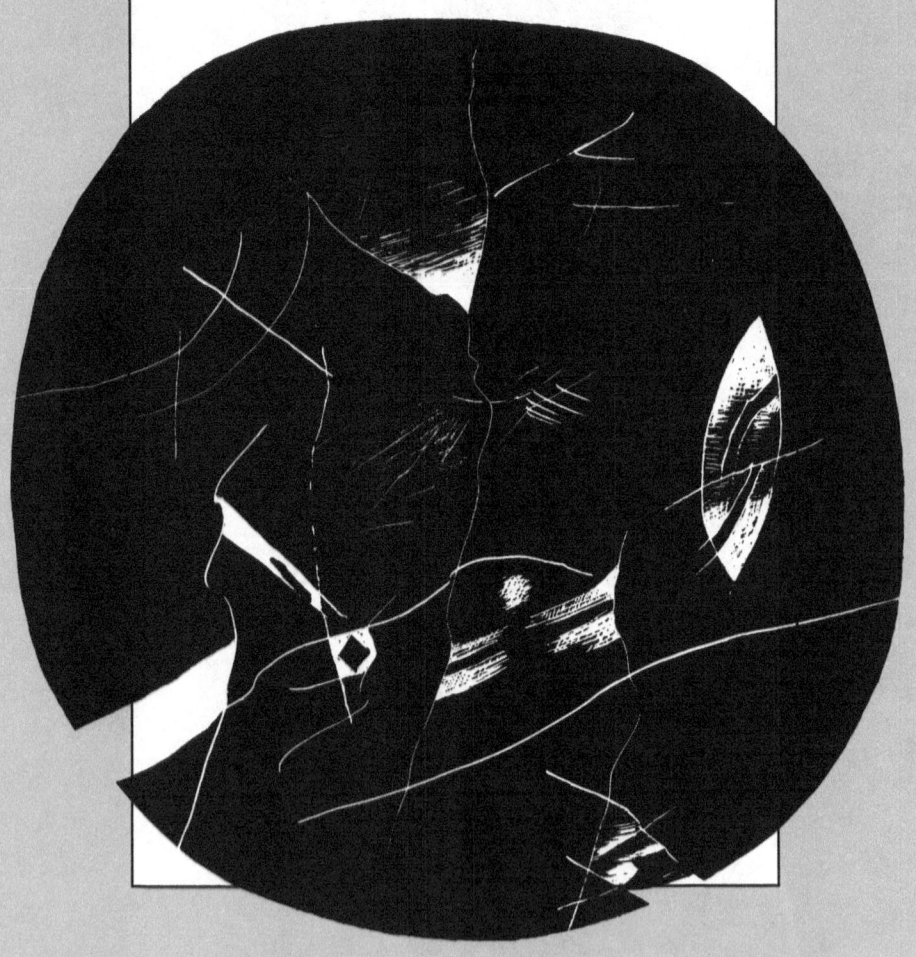

I WOULD TRAVEL but not be touched; I would move as if encased in crystal; I would see and experience the other lands aesthetically, as in a trance.

130.

*

I had a body of green and shimmering leaves; I drank the blue of skies and drank the red of blood which trickled from my mouth and ran all down my chest.

I found a cold, steel bar at the bottom of a mummy case. The bar was filled with faint, shimmering motes of light. I picked it up and held it tightly in my hands, close to my body, stretched between my genitals and chin. I bent my head over it and poured energy like white fluid into it. I heated my solar plexus and sent energy surging and looping like red blood around the bar; I sent energy up from my phallus like a stream of hot, red light; and I let a golden ray stream out from my heart to strike the bar at the center.

Then the cold, steel bar tilled with a shining white light that did not fade. It opened like a door and I stepped for a moment through that doorway into the light.

Through that door I would travel but not be touched; as a tree in the lands beyond that door I would eat the sky, as a warrior there I would drink the blood, but all as one who travels in a crystal case.

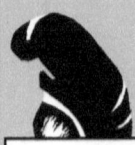
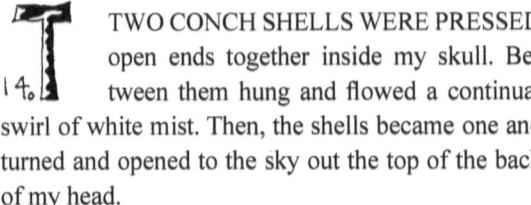
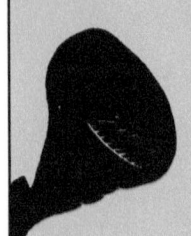

14.

TWO CONCH SHELLS WERE PRESSED open ends together inside my skull. Between them hung and flowed a continual swirl of white mist. Then, the shells became one and turned and opened to the sky out the top of the back of my head.

I saw a tree of tremendous height, the dark brown, vertical trunk and a few branches, but mostly only the multitude of blazing yellow leaves veined with red in autumn, reaching from far below to tower out of sight above. I knew the tree feeds me and I saw the red berries I eat, and I saw also that the great tree is a white bush and the berries are black.

I looked at the foot of the tree and the broad, shallow puddle of autumn rain gathered there; I came down close with my eye at the level of the leaves fallen in the water, to see them and the clouds reflected there as the water reached like a blue, calm ocean to the horizon with leaves and clouds shining in it like great ships. I travelled along the horizon to the right until I came to night and chains of stars and the moon all streaming down into the sea; but I did not then want the night and so I went back once more to the left, to the broad, cloud dappled, sunny autumn afternoon. I found a fountain there overflowing, and I rolled like a ball around and around splashing in the brimming pool at its base.

The back of my head opened to the future, like wings, like swimming, and I saw a book of sky blue and old, mottled buff paper with lines like pale pink stains. It was this book.

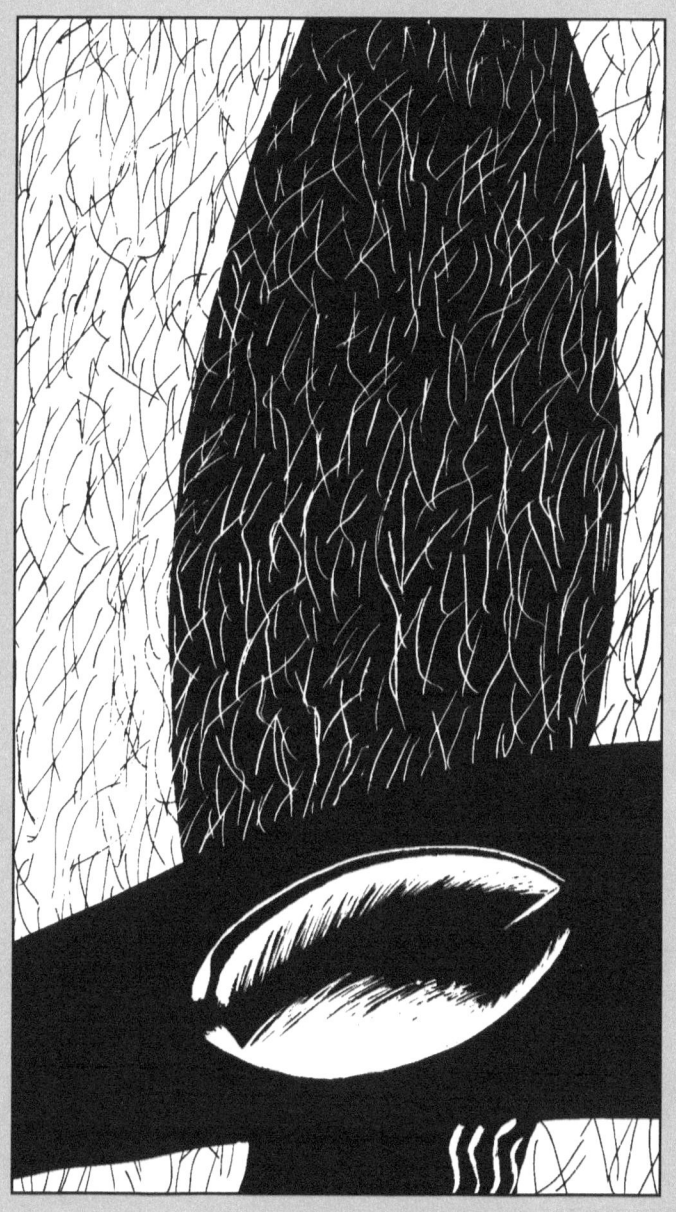

15. I WAS WALKING AGAIN on the lower stretches of the road leading up the black mountain, and came once more to the two stone gate posts. Conquering my earlier fears that dangerous ground might lie around the curve beyond the gate, I decided to enter. Just within the gate, I found the first of the loose black rocks. Most of the rocks were hemispherical, and there were positive and negative marks on their flat sides showing how once these opposite hemispheres had been joined as spheres. I held them high over my head and pressed them together in the way I thought they once had been, and a cone of sheets of white fire suddenly surrounded me.

*

I continued to ascend. The dark mountain rose out of sight on the right side of the road; on the left it fell steeply away to the valley below. A black slab of stone lay on the outer side of the road, and I was so high on the mountain that the slab seemed almost to lie against the sky. I put the black hemispherical rocks beneath the slab and pressed them together into a sphere. The slab became a dark skull of stone, and the cracks and holes and bumps in the stone were the runes that I must read. Afterward, I stood outside the gate at the bottom of the road; I looked back up where I had been and waited.

*

I was at the top of the mountain, and the top was marked with a silver cross set in black stone. I was black like the mountain and was winged like the giant Roc. I stood upon the cross and danced and spun upon

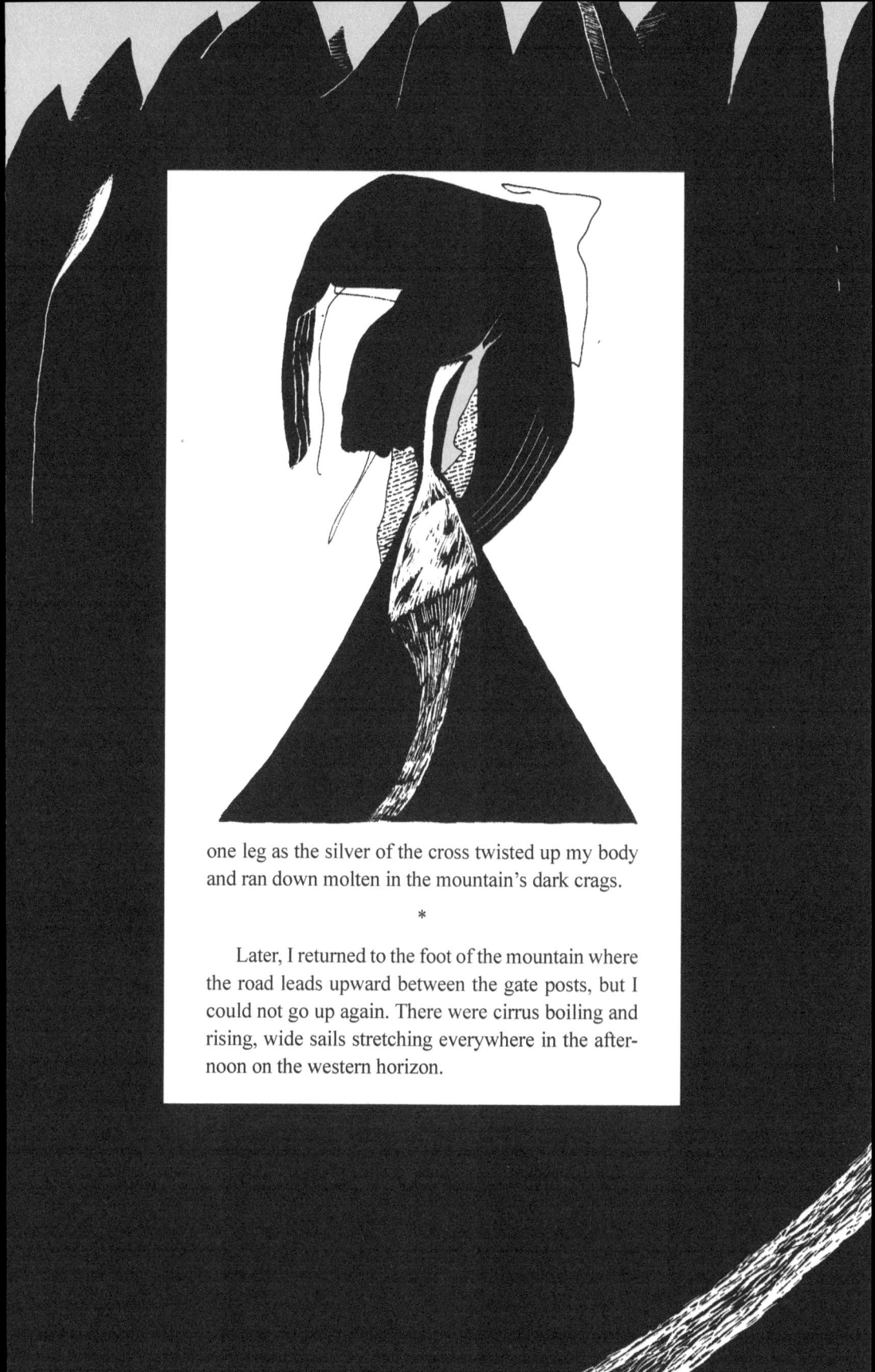

one leg as the silver of the cross twisted up my body
and ran down molten in the mountain's dark crags.

*

Later, I returned to the foot of the mountain where
the road leads upward between the gate posts, but I
could not go up again. There were cirrus boiling and
rising, wide sails stretching everywhere in the afternoon on the western horizon.

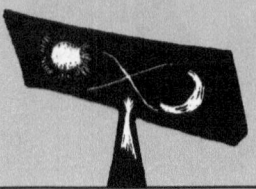

THEY SHOWED ME HOW TO USE
the energy of the conjunction of the sun
16. and moon, and said I should place that
powerful conflict far out above the horizon and let the
energy stream from it down to the plain in front of me,
where it would form a great, spinning ring of shimmering white light. They told me to put in the center of that ring whatever I would wish to understand
more fully.

I put in the ring a solitary star which I had seen
hanging over the ocean, and I saw in the star a spiral constantly rolling up everything together. The star
was all the while approaching me; and when it was
close, I saw that the spiral was a crystal shell. I saw
a pearl at the top of the lip of the shell, and from the
tight curled core of the shell I saw a stream of water
and light rain down upon the earth. They saw what I
had seen and told me to tell no one, because it was
only the design for the decoration on the base of a
statue yet to be made.

I took hold of the ring of light which comes from
the power of the conjunction of sun and moon, and
placed it around my body because I wanted my body
to become the statue for the base marked with the crystal shell. I worked the light of the ring with my hands, I
poured it on my genitals, I let it flow up into my head.

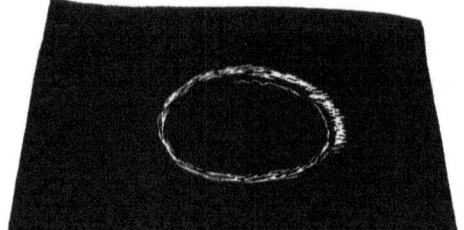

I was in the sea, and the long sweep of evening surf flowed like polished bronze between my head and groin. The crystal shell was on my forehead and the source of the All was in the little pearl on it; the pearl was the source of all the water and light that ran down from the eye of the spiral and rained everywhere upon the earth.

I stood at the shore of sunset and dawn, and was told to ascend the mountain there to learn what is carved upon its stones. The trail climbed into the afternoon and curved around the mountain's edge toward the side which faced the sea. A tree clung to rocks on the side of the mountain; it was silhouetted against the far, afternoon sky. I found a gold coin tangled in its roots, and the coin was marked with a half circle from which wavy lines fell and an arrow rose. I climbed on above the tree and found in the grass a paper bearing the word Love. When I reached the rocks at the top of the mountain, I found a pool among them and a shower of water falling into it from the crystal shell. The powerful splashing went right into my head and lifted me into the star which the shell had been in the beginning. I rested in a cabin in the star and wrote and drew on its walls this story of the climb.

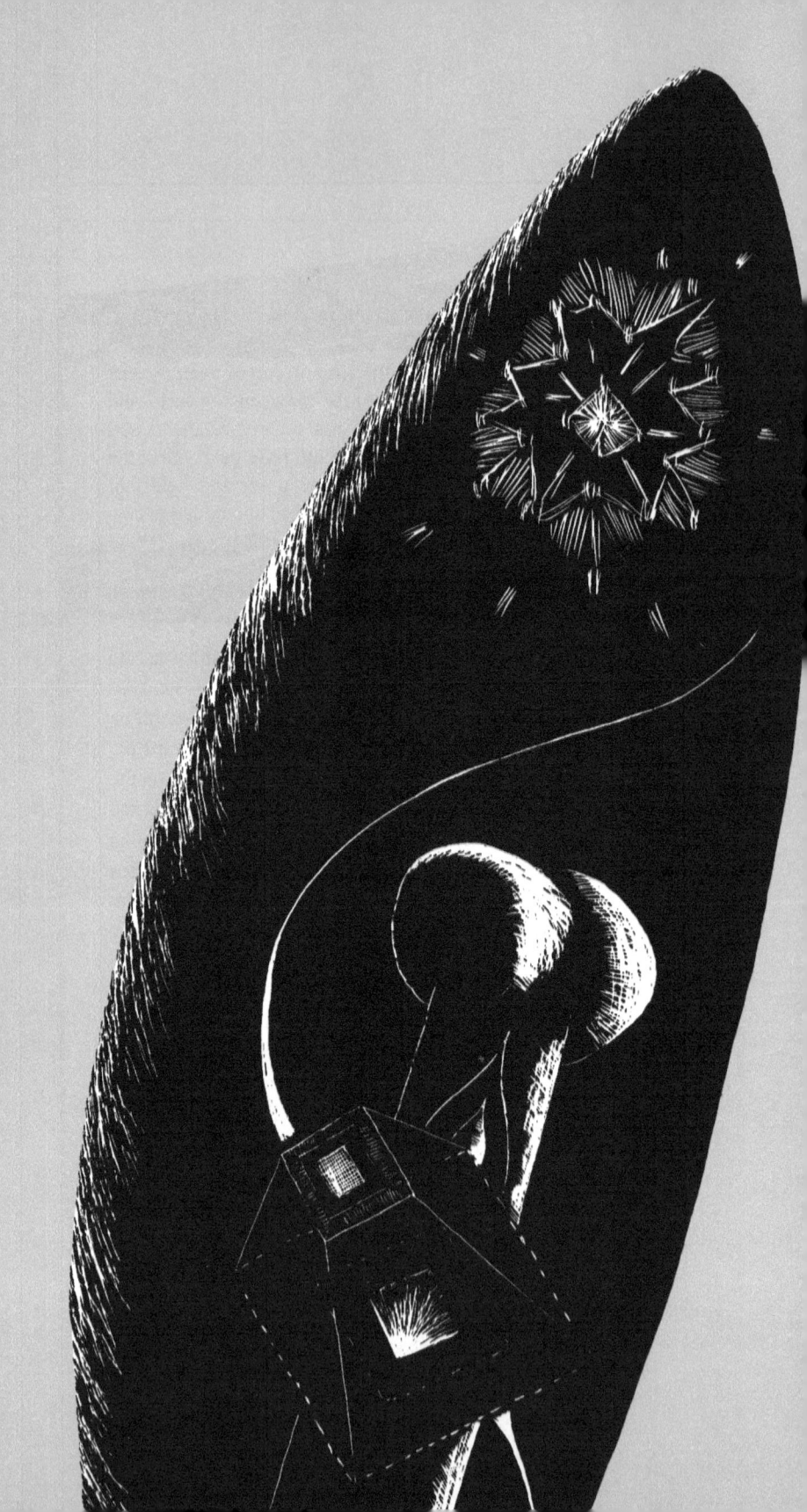

I RUBBED MY BODY all over with autumn flowers, I rubbed my cheeks with their dying petals, I rubbed my ears, arms, chest, nipples, belly, genitals. I rubbed my body everywhere with dry, flaking bits of blue, red, lavender and orange flowers. I was told to walk in the fields of grass growing on the high bluffs at the edge of the world. I ran my hands through the plants and varied grasses growing there, and I found a small, cellular chrysalis case far down among the stems.

I walked in the grass growing on the bluffs, and the wind blew on toward the edge of the world. I found a small, red, square amulet and hung it around my neck; I tattooed its sign into my chest right down to the bone because I was young with virile life.

I went on into the woods and became a satyr, mature and strong like the great wooden posts which mark the meeting and are the signs of the fertility of fields. There was a deep blue stone folded in the palm of my dark brown hand. I went out into the fields beyond the woods and wondered about the next, older age as a star opened, glittering and vibrating in my head.

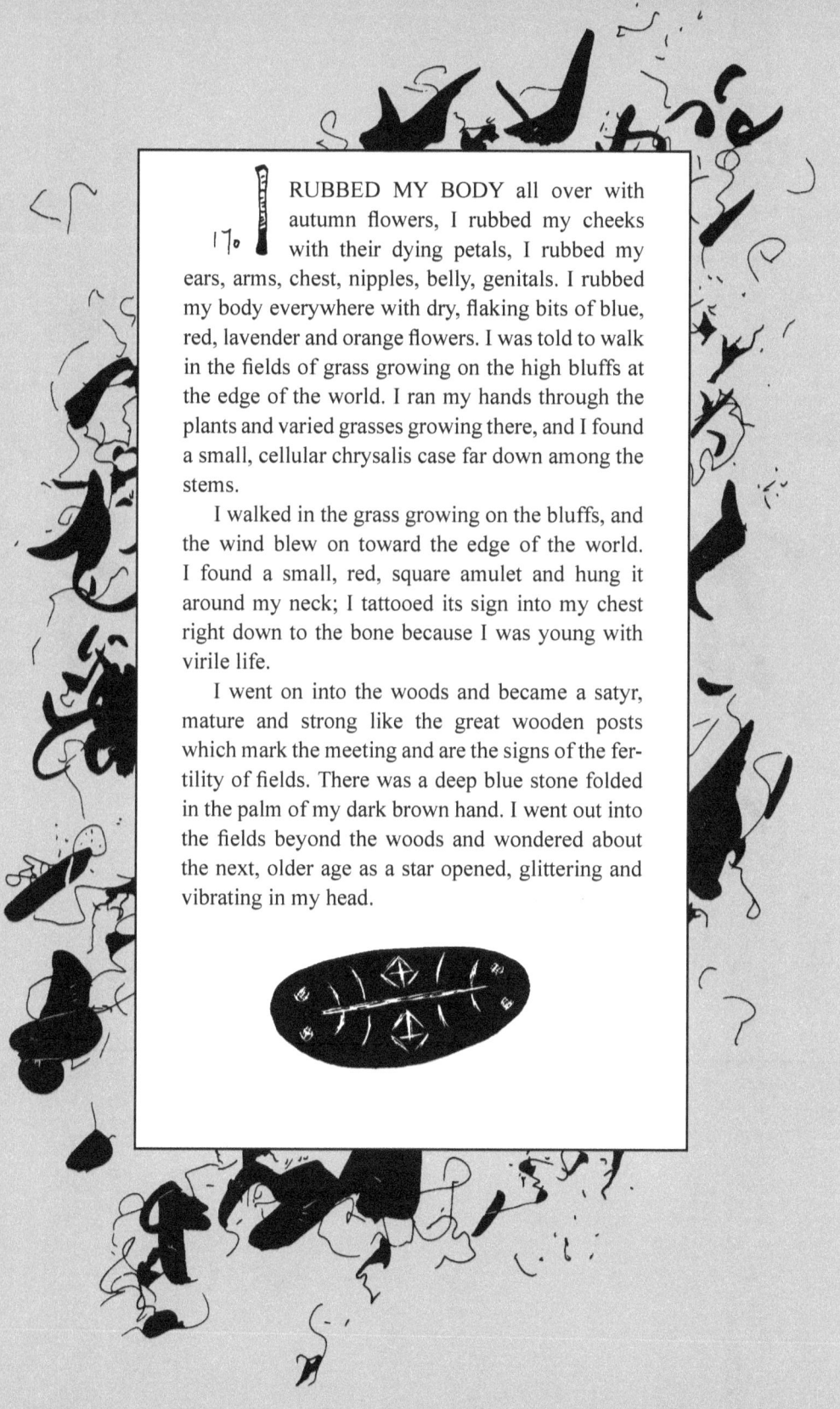

THEY TOLD ME THE BODY OF light which they had given me is a node of knowledge, a point of awareness in what they called "The Tissue of Infinity" that is the synthesis of mind and matter. They told me also that art is my tool for work beyond the grave, for finding the forms that are beyond death. They said that art is my tool for extraction of the essence, for cleansing from the husk, and for the study of all things in their aspect of geologic age. And then they said what I must do in these late autumnal days is to see in the flickering, shadowy sun of windless afternoons when all space vibrates between warm and cool, when every splash of sun opens and every stroke of shadow falls away, what I must do is to see through those openings of sun and shade, must see through them into the lands of art that are beyond the grave.

*

. . . only for a moment to Grandmother's house, to Grandmother's house I went, and her house was a cloudy sphere of blue crystal lying in brown autumnal grass.

*

They told me I have a crystal body energized by a ray from God. They said, although that body is always in me and always living, I am asleep to it and its life—and then they told me how to awaken.

They sent me walking on a long road curving among the hills toward the shore. They said I should meet my brother there and introduced me to a strong, brown, bearded man who slept in the lee of a hill just before the road made a last turn to the ocean beyond.

They led me down the beach to a warm place just above the surf, spread a carpet marked with a pattern of the intercourse of the sun and the moon, and told me to lie down on the carpet in the sun and sound of the sea. They laid a crystal on my belly and bade me think of it.

They said my physical body is the antenna, the lens which collects and through which passes the power of God. They said my body will collect the power and pass it to a crystal in front of my solar plexus, and the crystal will begin silently to reverberate with God's power, with his ray, and then the ray will reverberate my body ever more powerfully. They told me that with every breath the power enters my body to be concentrated in the crystal, and when the crystal begins to shine I should pass the crystal through all parts of my body in order to vibrate my crystal body and awaken me to its life. When I am fully awake to the life of my crystal body, they said, give it this silver locket of the sun and moon to wear and send it to walk nude and strong in the bright and windy surf.

They gave me a drawing tool for the crystal body to use for measure and study and projection of the things in its world, and they said the crystal body may when it needs help ask God to write in the book of lessons. And they said I may when I need joy, walk as the crystal body on plains and hills and clouds from horizon to zenith.

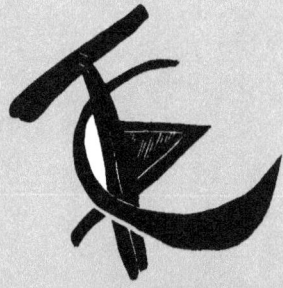

I WAS SHOWN the ring of the horizon, and was told, "They are waiting for you," There was a path wandering out to the edge, and I could see distant gleams there and obscure forms at the bottom of the sky.

19.

The flooding began to spread outward from a mounded, bubbling core. I came closer to the core and saw it was a mound/mountain of gold and jade. I thought the cabin in the star for which I have been searching might be on the mountain and so I came closer yet. The cabin was there and I entered because I wanted to see the pictures on the walls. One showed a temple in the mountains and I was in a room of it with a great waterfall streaming silently from heaven to earth close outside the window behind me. I knew then that the cabin in the star is close to the source of the waters of life.

There was a kite shaped like a skull flying from the roof of the cabin, blowing high in the wind with a long silvery tail blowing up from it toward the stars in a wind of stars; and I knew that the cabin in the star is my skull and the things I seek are painted there.

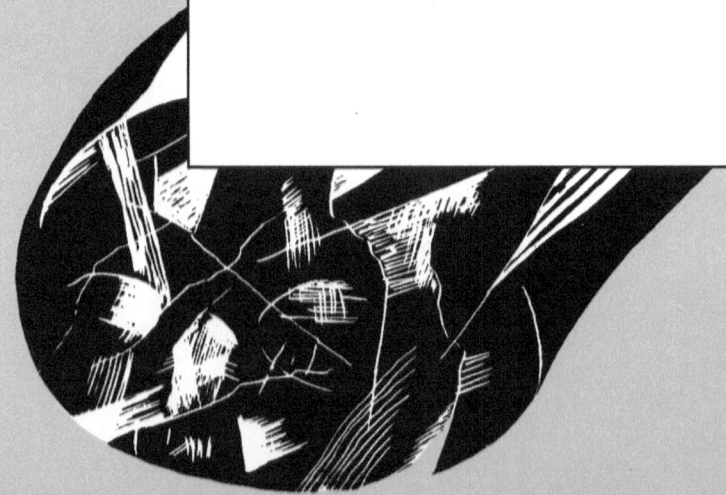

THERE ARE THREE RED LANDS. One is the rose-red land beyond the sunset. It is signalled by the blue-red colors of the sunset paradise. It has white crackling in it.

20.

The second is the red land of the earth, of old canyons where the sea dried away long ago. It is colored the red of ancient cities of the desert, of Petra, of Alexander's lost cities on the Oxus, of the seven cities of Cibola which Coronado never found. It is the red land through which flows the Blue River of Paradise.

The third is the red land of every human body, that thousand-voiced city, the continent of all who have ever lived and who whisper forever in the blood of everyone.

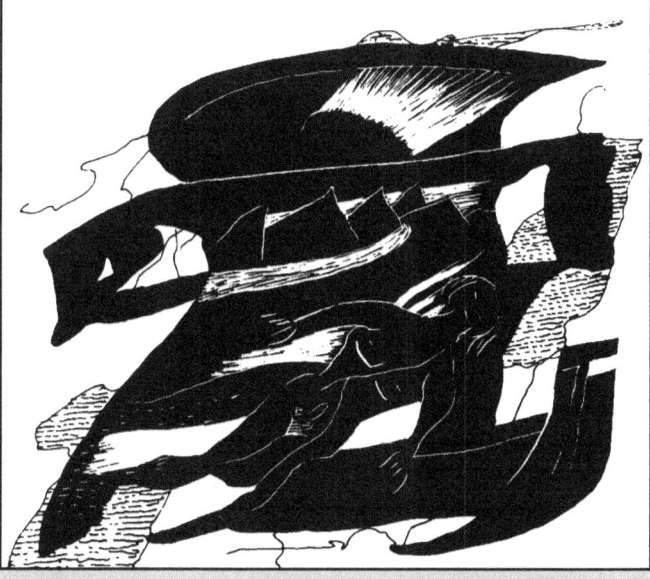

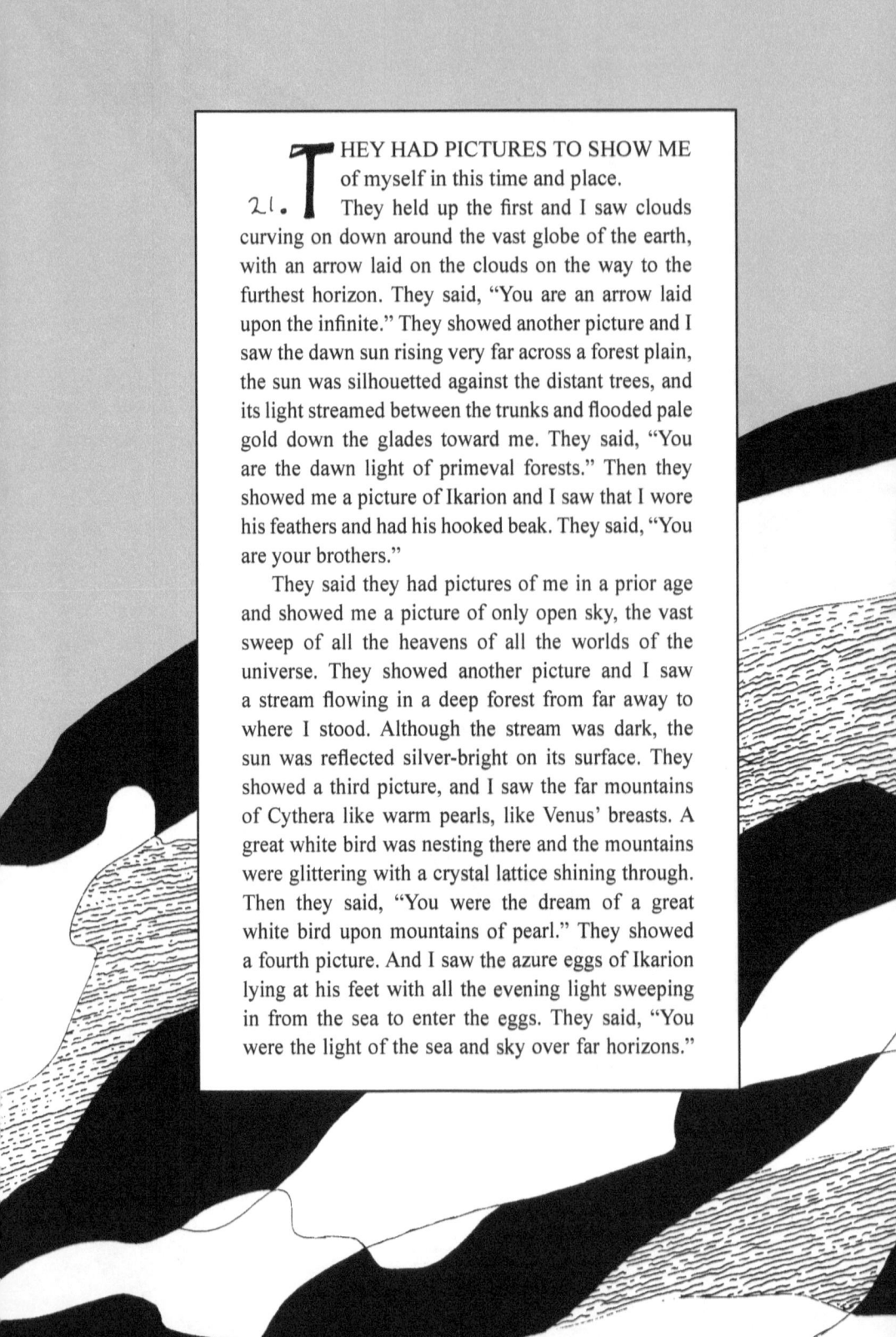

THEY HAD PICTURES TO SHOW ME of myself in this time and place.

21.   They held up the first and I saw clouds curving on down around the vast globe of the earth, with an arrow laid on the clouds on the way to the furthest horizon. They said, "You are an arrow laid upon the infinite." They showed another picture and I saw the dawn sun rising very far across a forest plain, the sun was silhouetted against the distant trees, and its light streamed between the trunks and flooded pale gold down the glades toward me. They said, "You are the dawn light of primeval forests." Then they showed me a picture of Ikarion and I saw that I wore his feathers and had his hooked beak. They said, "You are your brothers."

They said they had pictures of me in a prior age and showed me a picture of only open sky, the vast sweep of all the heavens of all the worlds of the universe. They showed another picture and I saw a stream flowing in a deep forest from far away to where I stood. Although the stream was dark, the sun was reflected silver-bright on its surface. They showed a third picture, and I saw the far mountains of Cythera like warm pearls, like Venus' breasts. A great white bird was nesting there and the mountains were glittering with a crystal lattice shining through. Then they said, "You were the dream of a great white bird upon mountains of pearl." They showed a fourth picture. And I saw the azure eggs of Ikarion lying at his feet with all the evening light sweeping in from the sea to enter the eggs. They said, "You were the light of the sea and sky over far horizons."

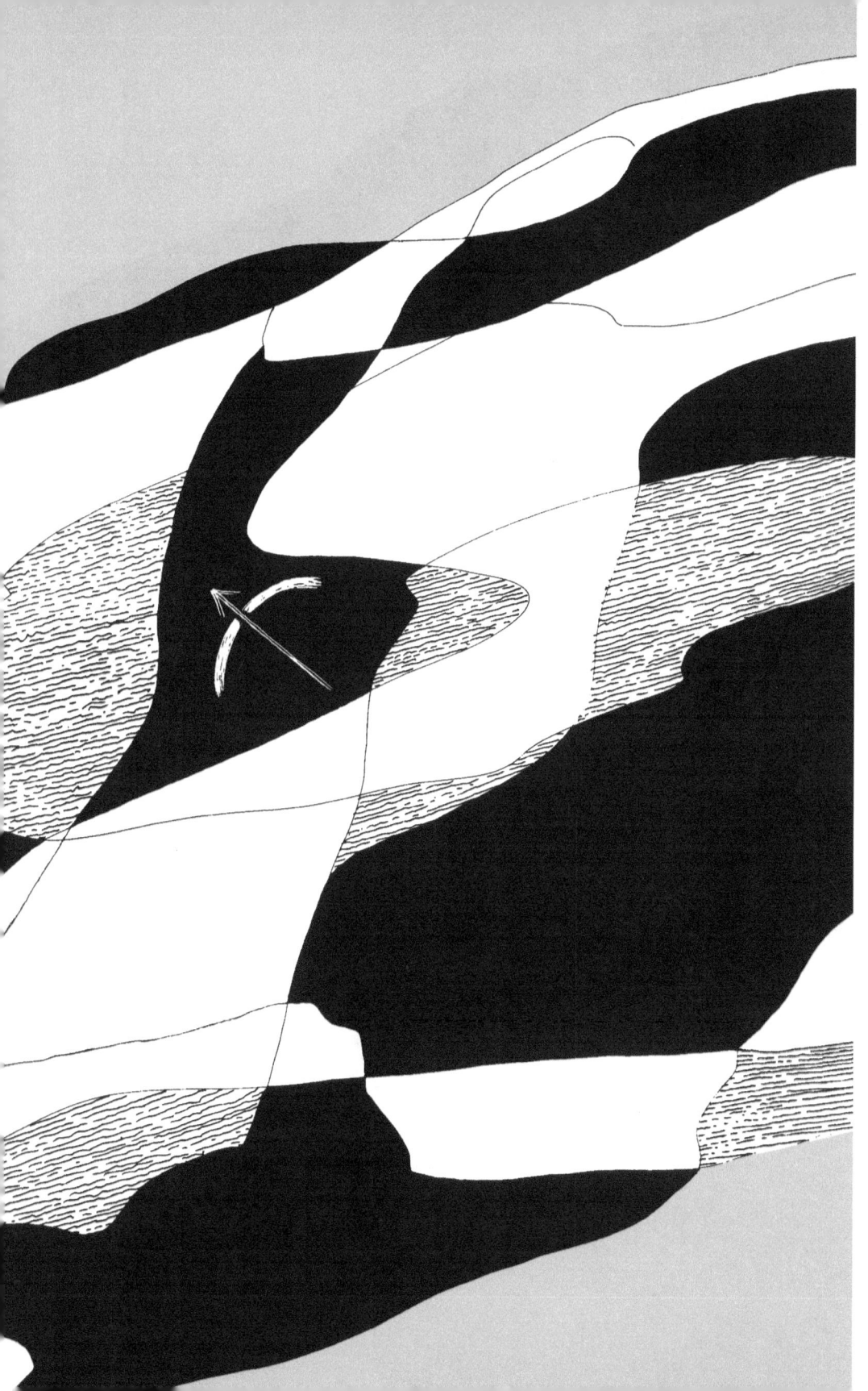

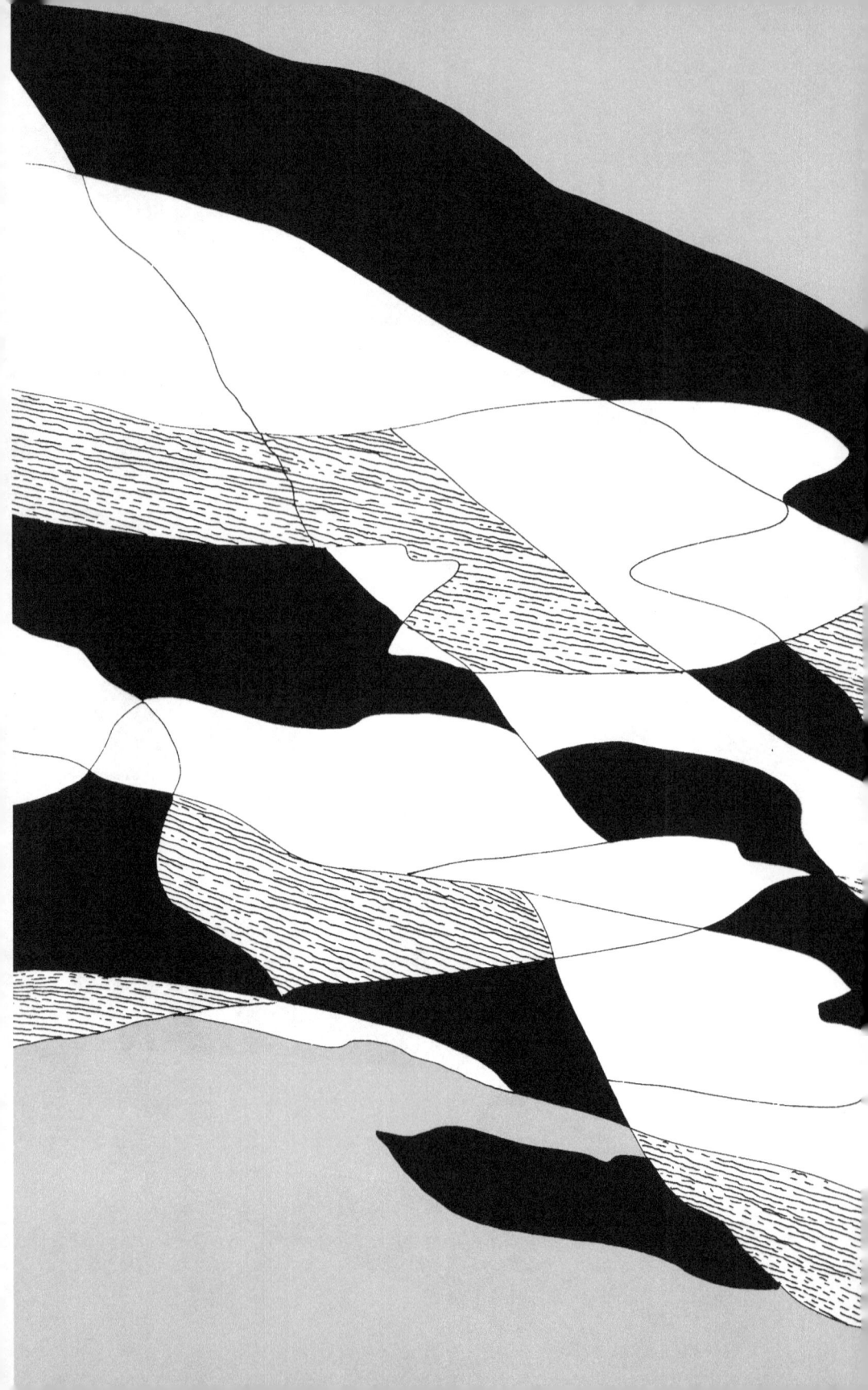

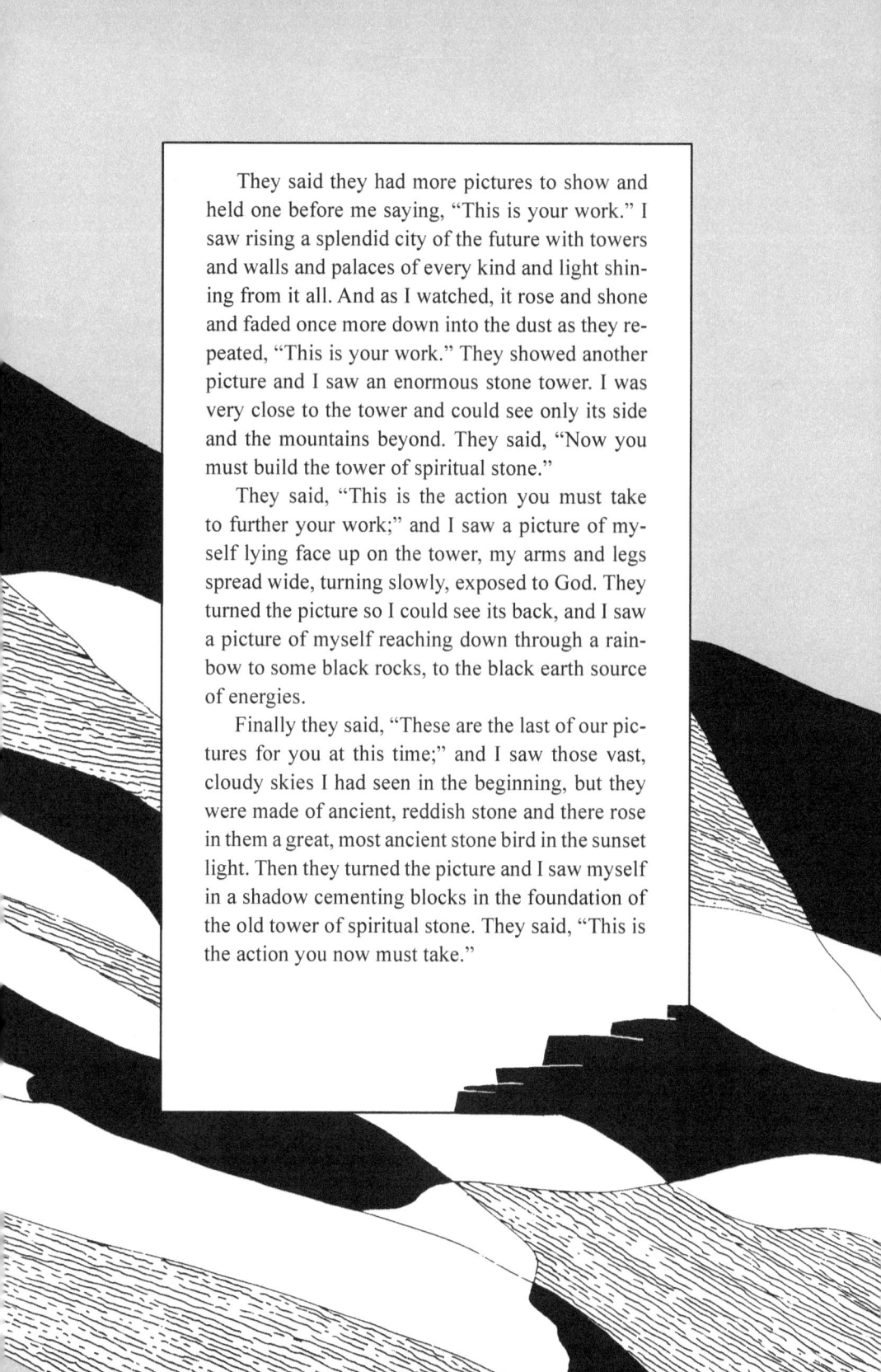

They said they had more pictures to show and held one before me saying, "This is your work." I saw rising a splendid city of the future with towers and walls and palaces of every kind and light shining from it all. And as I watched, it rose and shone and faded once more down into the dust as they repeated, "This is your work." They showed another picture and I saw an enormous stone tower. I was very close to the tower and could see only its side and the mountains beyond. They said, "Now you must build the tower of spiritual stone."

They said, "This is the action you must take to further your work;" and I saw a picture of myself lying face up on the tower, my arms and legs spread wide, turning slowly, exposed to God. They turned the picture so I could see its back, and I saw a picture of myself reaching down through a rainbow to some black rocks, to the black earth source of energies.

Finally they said, "These are the last of our pictures for you at this time;" and I saw those vast, cloudy skies I had seen in the beginning, but they were made of ancient, reddish stone and there rose in them a great, most ancient stone bird in the sunset light. Then they turned the picture and I saw myself in a shadow cementing blocks in the foundation of the old tower of spiritual stone. They said, "This is the action you now must take."

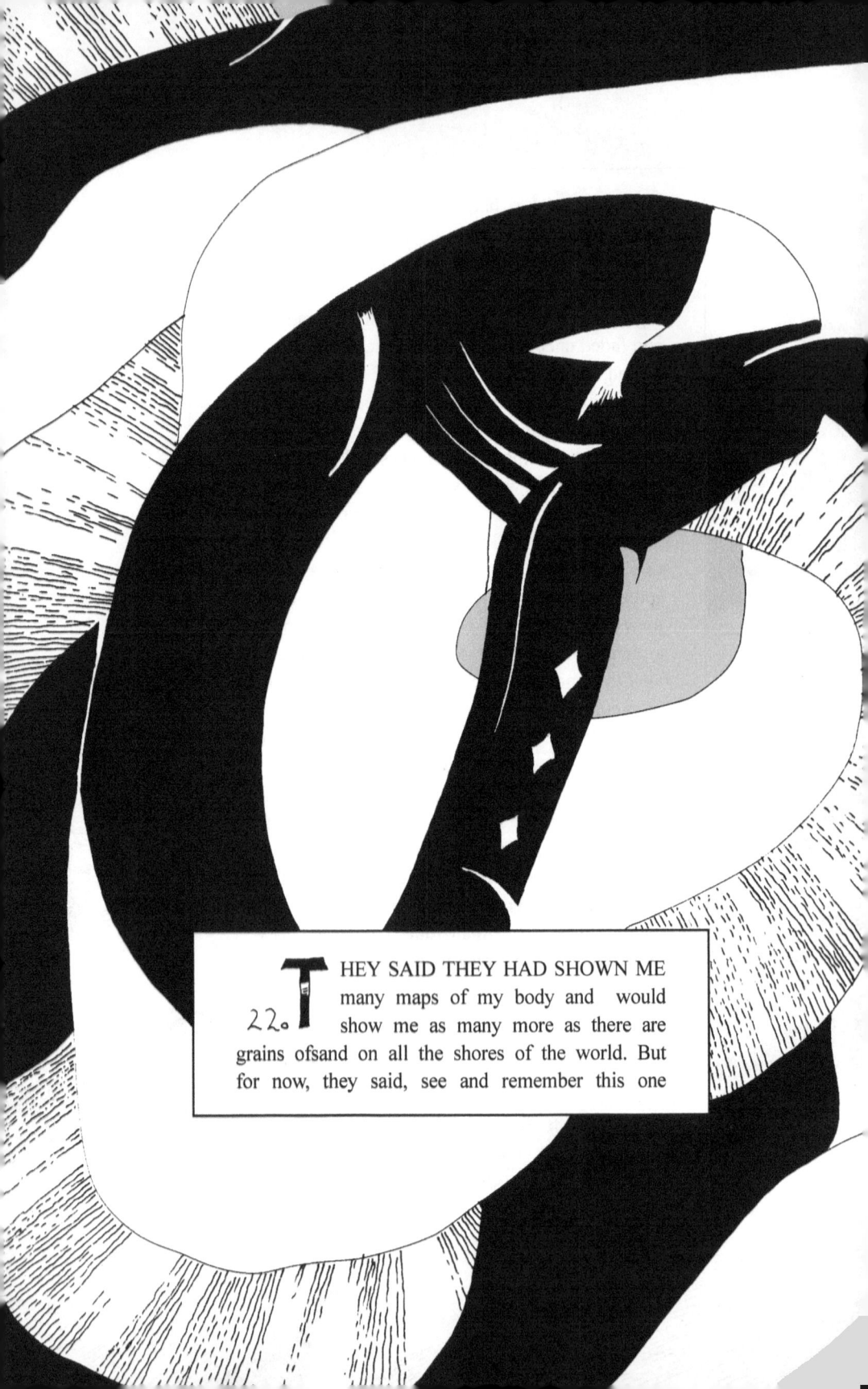

THEY SAID THEY HAD SHOWN ME many maps of my body and would 22. show me as many more as there are grains ofsand on all the shores of the world. But for now, they said, see and remember this one most, and they gave me an object they called a star tool. It consisted of a black rod with a row of glittering stars set in it and with black wooden wings extended from each side of the upper end. They told me to rub the star tool around the inside of my head, and it would open up the map of the constellations of the stars in my body.

I tried to count the stars on the tool but could not see to do it accurately. Then I used the tool as they had instructed, whirling it around and around in my head. The glittering stars rubbed from within against the outer edges of my brain, and the stars went all through my head as if they were on a chain passing through most complex gears. The fire of the energy of the stars spun out on a horizontal plane in my head and pressed, flashing against the inside of my skull. I put a star against the sole of each foot and two powerful currents of star energy came up my legs to meet in my crotch, I put a star in each testicle and one in my penis; star energy shone out where my genitals had been. I lay stars on my belly and they spun into a double star snake spiralling into the center. I sent stars to my heart from outside my body, and one clung and shone at the top and bottom of each side of the heart. And then I hung a star in each lobe of my brain and their lights shone out in great space. When I tried to look out, all the world was filled with star light.

But then all the gems lifted above me and became a single, massive gem of light, descending now to rest on the top of my head and sending long rays of golden light down through my body, rays sweeping down through the left, the right, the back. And then they told me that this has been the map of my body that leads my soul upward to the light, to be irradiated by the light.

I thanked them for this map of myself as a star, but asked also if I might not have a map of the place where my star body lives.

They gave me a sphere. I was placed at the center of it and told that this is the world of my experience as it is known from within, I looked up and saw a gear turning at the top of the axis of the sphere, directly above my head. The gear was made of brass punched with a ring of twelve circular holes. People sat on top of the gear, dangling their legs down through the holes. I was told these people are those beings who live in the sun whom I had begged to meet once long ago. I reached my hand as far as I could to the right and touched a bursting, spinning nebula of expanding star energy; I reached my hand as far as I could to the left and touched a sucking, spiralling contracting hole of blackness. I looked down and saw my genitals, tubes winding and tangling down, all hollow. I looked ahead of me and saw a bow and arrow, and remembered I had once been told, "You are an arrow laid upon the Infinite." I looked down again and saw far down in the tubes of my genitals the dark waters of evening flowing and foaming gently in a spring beneath black stones. I looked in back of me, and saw all the layers of earth above that spring beneath the stones; and I climbed the layers of earth until the geologic-eternal landscape opened out in a vast plain marked with ancient, blue-black mountains in a land of sunset red. And then I looked at the center, where my head was at the jeweled pivot center of the axis of this whole, slowly turning sphere.

And then I asked to see the cosmos in which this sphere of my life is placed. They put me in a wide, high sphere where there were at the top not only turning, glittering stars in all their geometric forms, but also thick, boiling and streaming afternoon cirrus. Far on the right was an ancient forest, and I was led to rub against the bark and catch and eat the leaves with my hands. Directly below was a deep, black, heaving ocean stretched as far as the eye could see, and I saw that it was also dark well with stars reflected in it. I knew I had been in that well before, with my arms and legs spread wide, lying on my back and turning slowly while I watched the heavens. The rim of the well was a silver snake and the well itself was a tube. The tube led around, up in back of me to where there was only the vast scarp of a mountain, scarred and marked with trilobites from the days before time began.

And then they showed me the far left quarter ot the cosmos in which I live, and I saw there in the sky a winged heart in flames. The red of the heart was the long red light beyond the horizon over the sea, and in those furthest clouds I held the hand of my Beloved for we were but pale golden wraiths in a distant sky, in the heart light of eternity. We were the song that whispers there forever in the land beyond death's bourne.

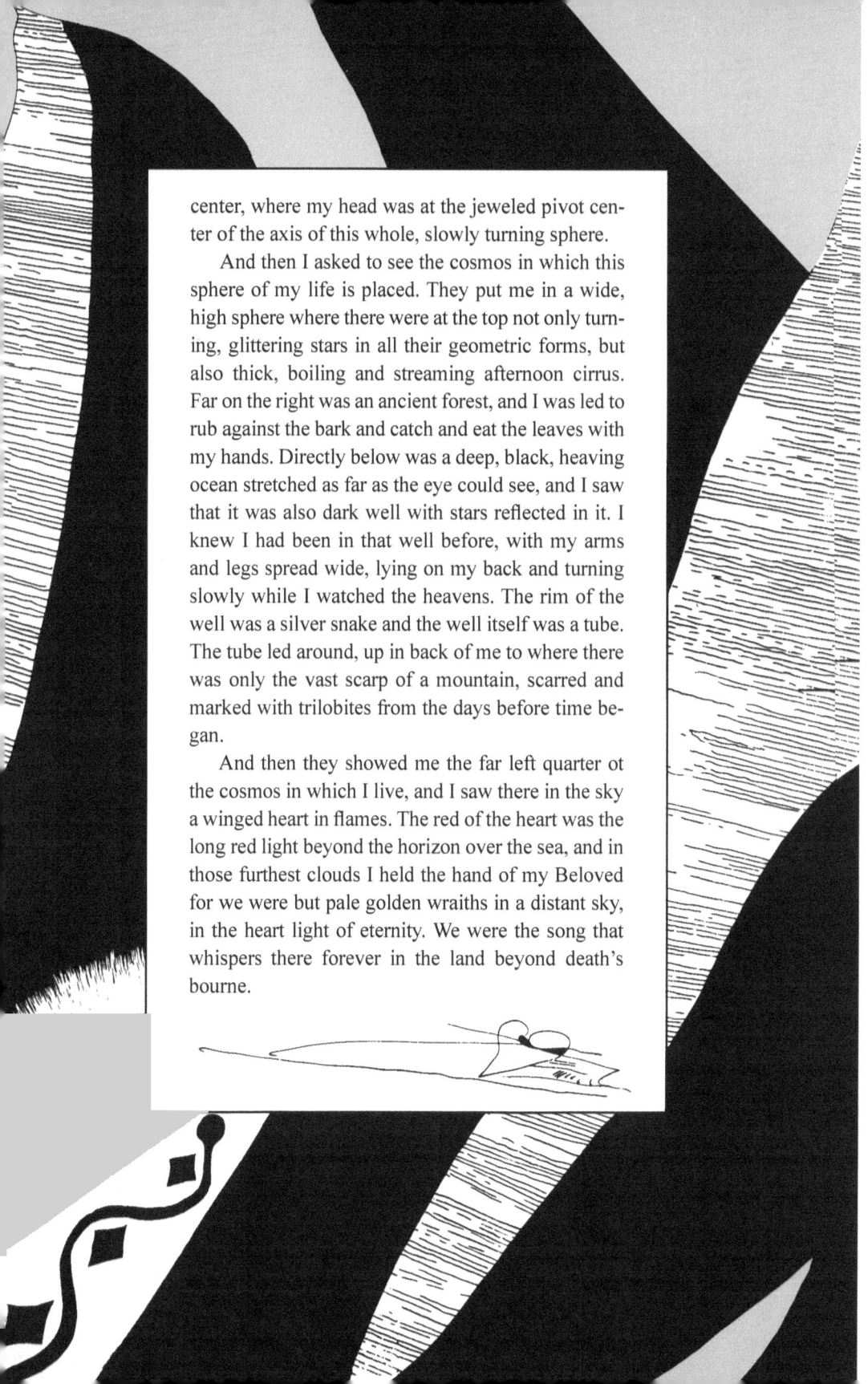

23. I WAS SENT ON two journeys to the further borders of the antique land. The first journey was to the Dawn Mountains of the Sunset. They were tall, triangular, sharp and flat like backdrops for a play. They were black, were crested with snow and outlined in orange light. There was a circular lake of very deep blue water at their foot with four rivers flowing into it. I was told it was the Uroboros Lake, and when I looked there was a circular snake in the center. Water and air seemed to stream down in a vortex in the middle of the circle of the snake, and far down in the glittering liquid I saw a ring. I was told it was the ring of the sun and moon and that I could not have it.

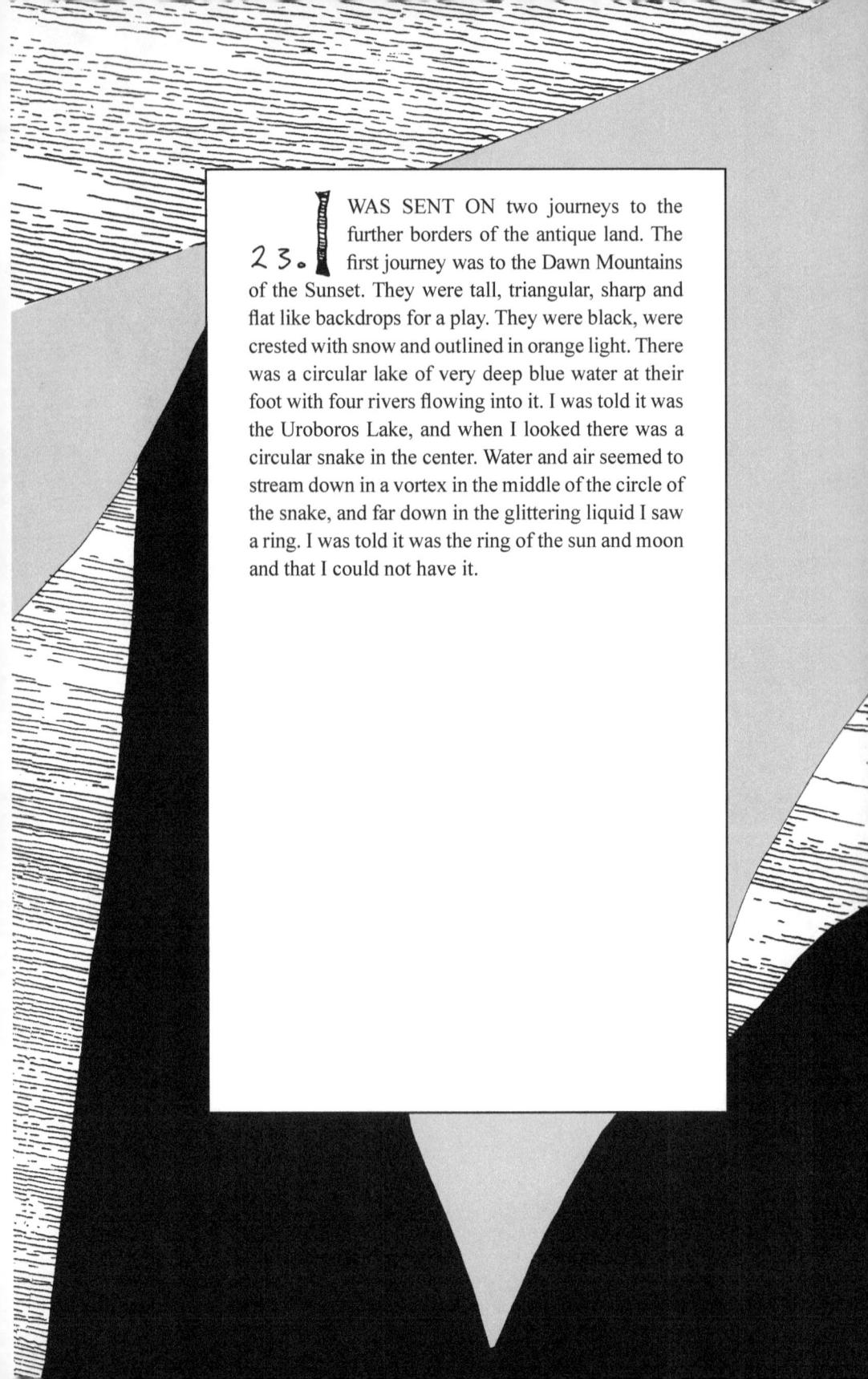

Then they said that since I had seen the furthest place at the back of the antique land, I should now see the highest one. They took me and spun me and swept me up to the palaces of Ikarion, where I was a shining blue sphere. But they said that was not high enough and so they lifted me higher, where I opened like a flower shone upon by a ring of white light above.

There was a speck of black dirt or a worm on one of my petals and the message came down from that ring that I must burn away the dirt in myself. The flower closed into the blue sphere, and I spun very hard indeed to burn away the speck.

I went back up as a flower to expose myself once more to the white radiance of God ; and while I was there, suddenly, buds were lifting and opening everywhere in waves on a great plain that swept to the horizon.

After a time, I was brought down from the heights. I was told that all the buds were my works. I thanked God for these works. I was told all the buds were also my children, and I thanked God also for them.

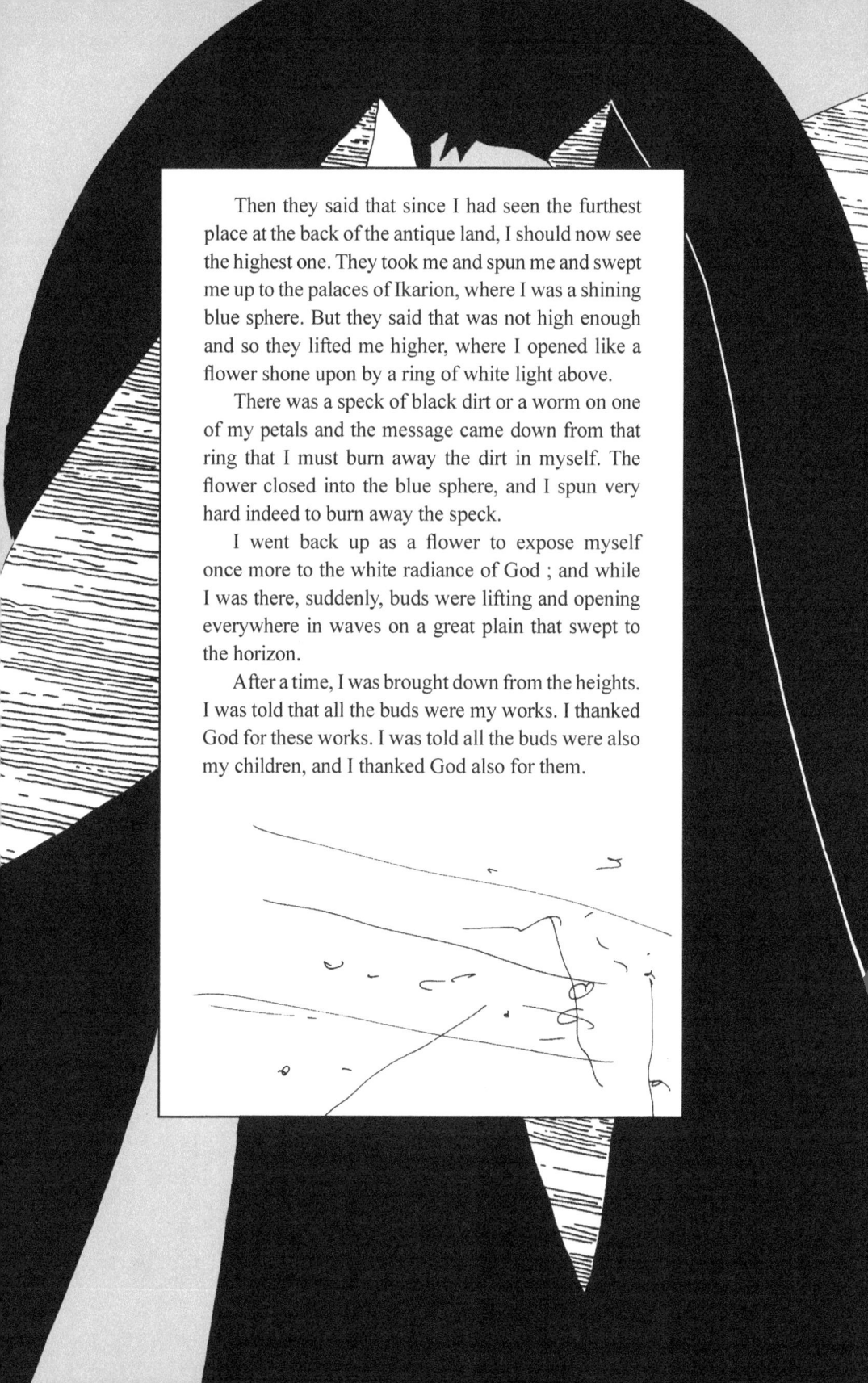

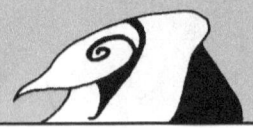

24. **T**HEN I ASKED THE TO SEE THE origins of all things, and a very little boy came to lead me up a beach to where rocky cliffs came out against the surf. I was afraid the boy would be hurt by the waves when we came to the rocks at the end of the beach, but he insisted I go on without him and pointed up to a gate at the top of the cliffs whence white light streamed down flooding, clinging to his hand. The little boy and I played together for a time at the base of the dark cliffs, running our fingers over the runes carved there, until at last I could wait no longer but knew I must go upward to the gate.

I flew clumsily, a dark bird with white wings, on up the line of cliffs toward the gate at the top where the light was a stream of flickering colors like a waterfall. I went to the top of the fall where the light poured over a bar held up by three interlocked rings and with a post at each end surmounted by a ring. I climbed one of the posts. It was also a stone bird and the ring was a golden collar around its neck. I knew my flight is always heavy until God makes light my wings, and so I clung to the neck of the stone bird with my right arm and dipped my left hand into the stream so the river of colors and flames and lights could flow in me.

Afterward, thanking God for his gift, I went back down to the beach and met the little boy once more. He pointed to himself, to the light in the gate and to me. I knew we three are one.

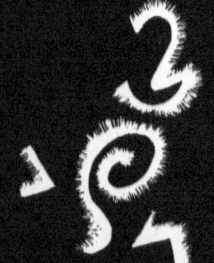

25. NEAR THE MOUNTAIN, and then going down by the lake I met the little boy again, the very little child who had led me on the walk up the beach to where the rocks are carved with runes and who pointed to the gate of the origin. This time, he showed me a chain, and I was standing between my father and my son, my grandfather beyond my father, my grandson beyond my son . . . and they were in a semicircle with ends extended infinitely. I was in the center, turning and dancing before them, pirouetting and touching the ground at every cardinal point.

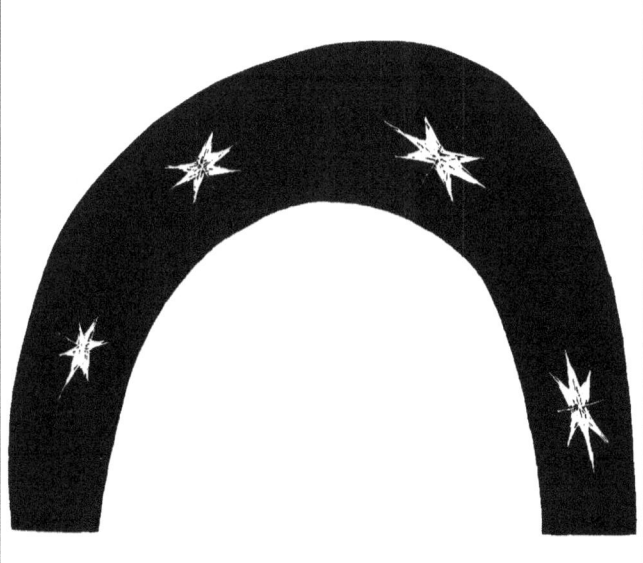

26. CLUNG TO STEEP mountain rocks, but was unable to climb further to the high place where I could see all light flashing in downward curves. There were people sitting up there, looking out to the farthest spaces which show no clear horizon or limit. They said someday I might be with them and look out through their eyes.

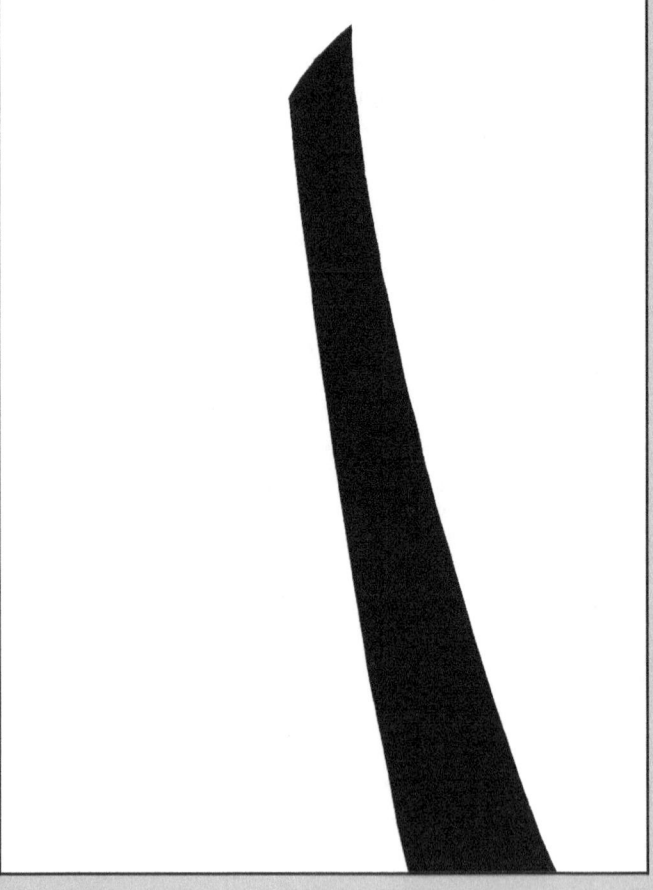

*T*HE MOON HUNG CLOSE, huge and dark over the land; a few black rocks 27. stood high against its silvery new edge. I clung to the rocks near the western crest of Tamalpais, holding against the wind sweeping in from the sea. I looked out across the evening and saw the white surf far below and a mist rising slowly over the lagoon, drifting down the valley, spreading over the shore.

I saw the mist spread like a great disc turning slowly and spiralling inward and plummeting downward at the center who knew how far. I was told mind is a mist over the sea.

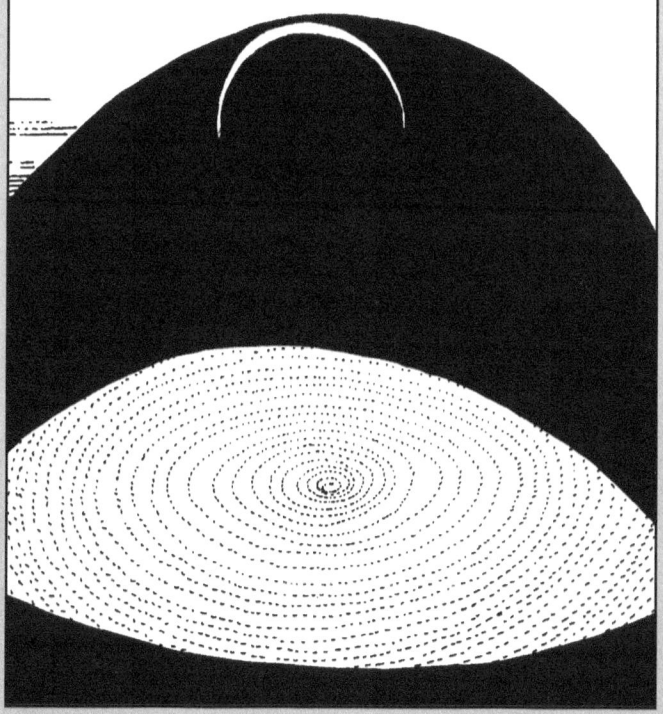

28. THREE DOORS OPEN on the timeless. *Memory* is the key to the door marked Past that opens on the timeless; *Now* is the key to the door marked Present that opens on the timeless; and *Prophecy* is the key to the door marked Future that opens on the timeless. I went with those keys through mountains where there is no snow, the mountains where once long ago I went to dwell with my Beloved. I saw a sarcophagus and remembered I had been told that art is my tool for work beyond the grave, and so I knew that art is also my work beyond time because death is the boundary of time.

Far among the peaks I saw the way beyond the mountains. It was a shining bright disc that stood upright like a vast, rising sun between two peaks. There was a broad triangular opening pointing down from the top to the bottom of the disc, and a river flowed from it. I heard them say I had gone into the timeless long ago, for I came from God and to God I will return.

Then from the white light of the heights they made a ring to be worn where my wedding ring is. The ring was of gold with a turquoise stone carved as a scarab which was a trilobite which was a cicada. They touched my forehead and my hands with strong beams of the white light from which they had made the ring.

*

On the morning of my last day travelling in the antique land, I lay upon the grass and found that the point of light lay nearest to my heart. I lifted the point out of my body and vibrated my heart with it, then my solar plexus and then my genitals. My mind directed the action, my mind felt the results. I massaged my phallus with the point of light and rubbed the sperm on my heart; my solar plexus glowed warm like the sun with four ways meeting in it; and my heart became a brighter, more transparent red and its wings and bindings a brighter gold. I swallowed the green point of light and carried the life of grass and trees all through my body; I swallowed the purple point and carried the power of the joined ends of the spectrum all through me also. I knew this was to be my last day in the antique land, and so I stretched and stretched along the horizons of the place, to perceive and remember all that which I had found there but would not see again.

And then they said, "Walk on into the future."

*

. . . the Stream of my spirit flew far in the pale cerulean beyond the clouds; it curved down the sky toward the setting sun; it was a shining line with wings at its head twisting and beating far, far down toward the sun, glowing in its rays.

*

. . . and in the evening I watched the speckled twilight fade beyond Tamalpais. I smelled the wind of distant skies and knew the source of all my food is always there.

There is a cabin in the evening star. The walls are hung with pictures, the shelves are lined with books. This has been drawn from those pictures; it has been told from those books.

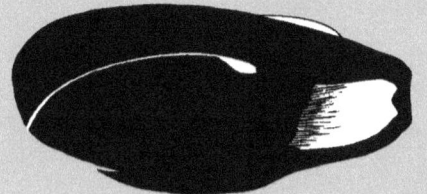

www.ingramcontent.com/pod-product-compliance
Lightning Source LLC
Chambersburg PA
CBHW021024180526
45163CB00005B/2108